W9-BYH-572

How to Use

History Pockets

History Pockets—Colonial America provides an exciting travel adventure back to the time of Pilgrims, hornbooks, and new settlements. The engaging activities are stored in labeled pockets and bound into a decorative cover. Students will be proud to see their accumulated projects presented all together. At the end of the book, evaluation sheets have been added for teacher use.

Make a Pocket

1. Use a 12" x 18" (30.5 x 45.5 cm) piece of construction paper for each pocket. Fold up 6" (15 cm) to make a 12" (30.5 cm) square.

2. Staple the right side of each pocket closed.

3. Punch two or three holes in the left side of each pocket.

Assemble the Pocket Book

1. Reproduce the cover illustration on page 3 for each student.

2. Direct students to color and cut out the illustration and glue it onto a 12" (30.5 cm) square of construction paper to make the cover.

3. Punch two or three holes in the left side of the cover.

4. Fasten the cover and the pockets together. You might use string, ribbon, twine, raffia, or binder rings.

Every Pocket Has...

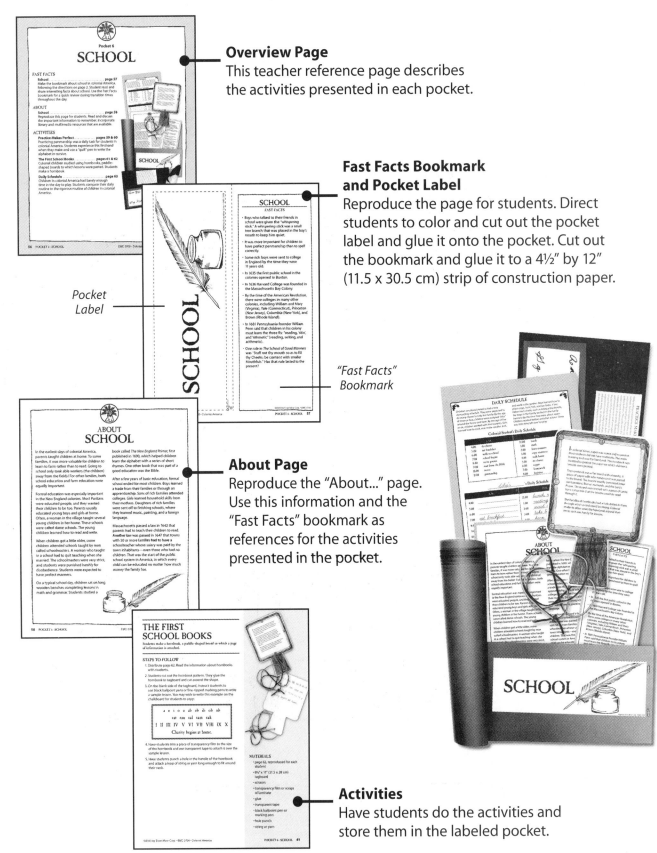

Overview Page
This teacher reference page describes the activities presented in each pocket.

Fast Facts Bookmark and Pocket Label
Reproduce the page for students. Direct students to color and cut out the pocket label and glue it onto the pocket. Cut out the bookmark and glue it to a 4½" by 12" (11.5 x 30.5 cm) strip of construction paper.

Pocket Label

"Fast Facts" Bookmark

About Page
Reproduce the "About..." page. Use this information and the "Fast Facts" bookmark as references for the activities presented in the pocket.

Activities
Have students do the activities and store them in the labeled pocket.

EMC 3709 • Colonial America • ©2003 by Evan-Moor Corp.

Note: Reproduce this cover for students to color, cut out, and glue to the cover of their Colonial America book.

COLONIAL AMERICA

Name:

©2003 by Evan-Moor Corp. • EMC 3709 • Colonial America

Pocket 1 • INTRODUCTION TO

COLONIAL AMERICA

FAST FACTS

Colonial America . . . . **page 5**
Make the bookmark about colonial America, following the directions on page 2. Students read and share the interesting facts about colonial America. Use the Fast Facts bookmark for a quick review during transition times throughout the day.

ABOUT

Colonial America . . . . **page 6**
Reproduce this page for students. Read and discuss the important information to remember. Incorporate library and multimedia resources that are available.

ACTIVITIES

The Thirteen Colonies Time Line . . . . **pages 7 & 8**
Students put together a time line showing the European settlement of the thirteen colonies. Refer to this time line periodically throughout the unit.

Settling the Colonies Booklet . . . . **pages 9–11**
Reproduce pages for students. Read and discuss the information about the three geographical groups of colonies. Provide two 9" x 12" (23 x 30.5 cm) sheets of colored construction paper for each student to use as a cover for the information booklet. Have students glue the completed map from page 12 to the front of the booklet; staple the pages inside folder.

Map of the Thirteen Colonies . . . . **page 12**
Students study the map of the thirteen original colonies. They use colored pencils to shade in the colonies. Using references found in this pocket, students use light red for the New England colonies, yellow for the middle colonies, and light blue for the southern colonies.

Settling the Colonies, a Questionnaire . . . . **page 13**
Reproduce this page for students. Now that students have studied the three geographical groups of colonies, they are to choose which colony they would have settled in and fill out a questionnaire about their choice.

The Thirteen Colonies Word Search . . . . **page 14**
Students enjoy learning the names of the thirteen colonies as they complete a fun word search. An answer key is provided on page 96.

 EMC 3709 · Colonial America · ©2003 by Evan-Moor Corp.

INTRODUCTION TO
COLONIAL
AMERICA

©2003 by Evan-Moor Corp. • EMC 3709

COLONIAL AMERICA
FAST FACTS

• The thirteen colonies were divided into four geographical groups. They were (1) the New England, or northern colonies; (2) the middle colonies; (3) the Chesapeake colonies; and (4) the southern colonies. The Chesapeake colonies are now considered part of the southern colonies.

• Many northern colonists came to the New World in search of a separation of government and the Church.

• The middle colonies attracted the most diverse number of European ethnic groups—Dutch, English, French, German, Scottish, Irish, Swedish, and Welsh.

• By the mid-1700s there were more Africans living in some southern colonies than Europeans or Native Americans.

• In 1700 there were 250,000 people living in the thirteen colonies. By 1775 the population had grown to about 2.5 million.

• After the original thirteen colonies, the next states to be admitted to the Union were Vermont, Kentucky, and Tennessee.

• To symbolize the thirteen colonies, the Great Seal of the United States features an eagle and thirteen olive leaves, olives, arrows, and stars. The seal is now on the back of the dollar bill.

©2003 by Evan-Moor Corp. • EMC 3709

ABOUT
COLONIAL AMERICA

The story of the United States of America starts with the story of how very different people from several European nations, many African homelands, and hundreds of native tribes became thirteen American colonies.

Thousands of people lived in North America long before Europeans came. They were made of up many individual tribes, each with its own culture and language, but they are often referred to as a collective group. That group has many names: *Indians, American Indians, Native Americans, indigenous people,* and *Amerindians* are some of these names.

Many people from all over Europe came to the East Coast of North America. They all had their reasons. Some came for opportunities of owning their own land and businesses. Others came for the chance to live and worship as they chose, because they had experienced religious persecution back in Europe. The idea of self-government was very appealing to many. The Europeans had also heard that this vast new land had abundant natural resources.

Not all colonists came to the New World voluntarily. The slave trade brought people from Africa against their will to work as indentured servants and as slaves. Their contribution to the economy of the colonies was invaluable.

People settled in the northern or New England colonies, consisting of Connecticut, Massachusetts, New Hampshire, and Rhode Island. Others made their homes in the middle colonies, which were Delaware, New Jersey, New York, and Pennsylvania. They also settled in the southern colonies of Georgia, Maryland, North Carolina, South Carolina, and Virginia.

Each colony was different. They spoke different languages, practiced different religions, and had different customs. The one thing that united them was their loyalty to England. The colonists traded with England, and England protected them from other countries. This cooperation continued until the colonies grew tired of paying taxes to England. The colonists decided they wanted to govern themselves, so they united to defeat the British Empire in the American Revolutionary War. By 1776 the thirteen colonies were called the United States of America.

   EMC 3709 · Colonial America · ©2003 by Evan-Moor Corp.

THE THIRTEEN COLONIES TIME LINE

Students are about to travel back in time to the settling of the thirteen colonies by the Europeans. The first permanent settlement was in Virginia in 1607. Georgia was the last colony to be established in 1732.

Whenever dates are given throughout the unit, refer back to this time line to help students place the settlements chronologically.

MATERIALS

- pages 7 (bottom only) and 8, reproduced for each student
- scissors
- glue

STEPS TO FOLLOW

1. Students cut out the time line sections and glue them together.

2. As a class, read about the founding of the first permanent settlements of the thirteen colonies on the time line.

3. Fold the time line and store it in Pocket 1.

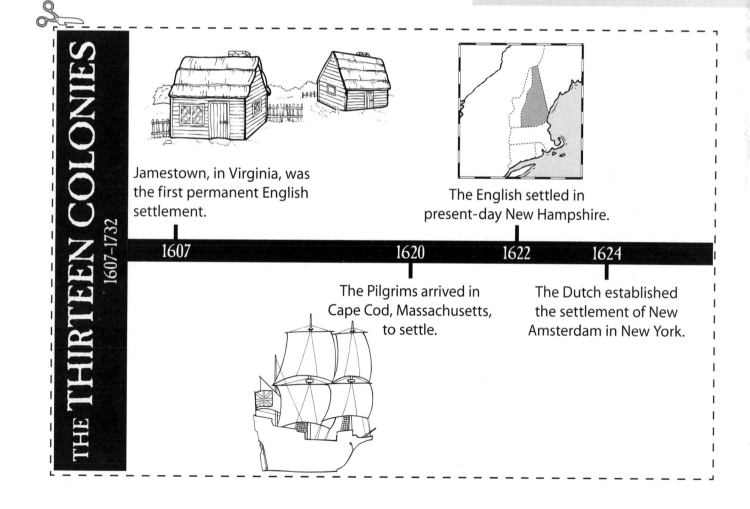

THE THIRTEEN COLONIES 1607–1732

Jamestown, in Virginia, was the first permanent English settlement.

The English settled in present-day New Hampshire.

1607   1620   1622   1624

The Pilgrims arrived in Cape Cod, Massachusetts, to settle.

The Dutch established the settlement of New Amsterdam in New York.

THE THIRTEEN COLONIES TIME LINE

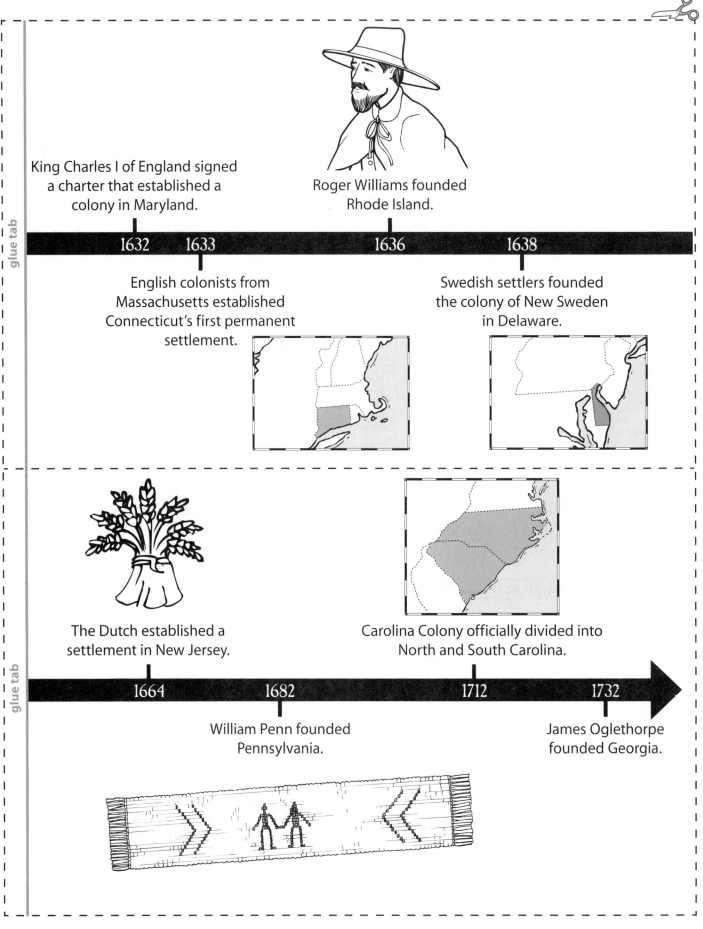

King Charles I of England signed
a charter that established a
colony in Maryland.

Roger Williams founded
Rhode Island.

1632   **1633**   **1636**   **1638**

English colonists from
Massachusetts established
Connecticut's first permanent
settlement.

Swedish settlers founded
the colony of New Sweden
in Delaware.

The Dutch established a
settlement in New Jersey.

Carolina Colony officially divided into
North and South Carolina.

1664   **1682**   **1712**   **1732**

William Penn founded
Pennsylvania.

James Oglethorpe
founded Georgia.

Note: Reproduce pages 9–11 for students to use with the "Settling the Colonies Booklet" activity, as described on page 4.

THE NEW ENGLAND COLONIES

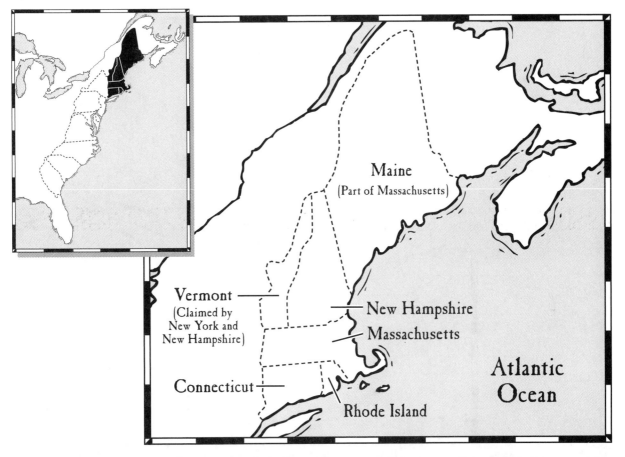

Colony (Year Founded)	Origin of Name	Chief Products
Connecticut (1633)	Algonquian Indian words meaning "on the long tidal river"	Farming (corn and wheat), fishing
Massachusetts (1620)	Massachuset Indian words meaning "near the great hill"	Farming (corn and cattle), fishing, lumbering, shipbuilding
New Hampshire (1622)	County of Hampshire in England	Farming (potatoes), fishing, textiles, shipbuilding
Rhode Island (1636)	Dutch words for "red island"	Farming (cattle and dairy), fishing, lumbering

THE MIDDLE COLONIES

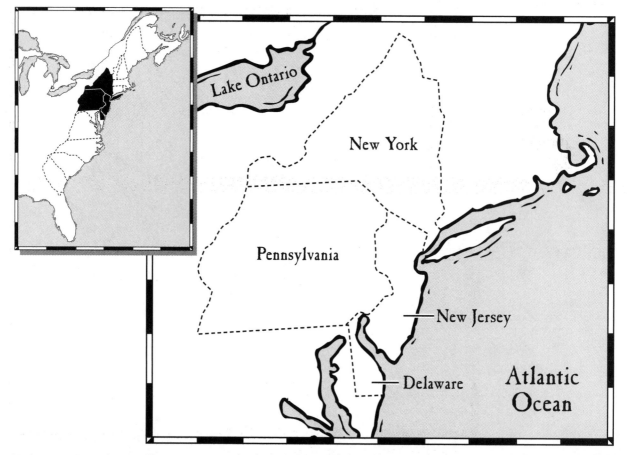

Colony (Year Founded)	Origin of Name	Chief Products
Delaware (1638)	Delaware tribe and early governor of Virginia, Lord de la Warr	Fishing, lumbering
New Jersey (1664)	Isle of Jersey in England	Ironworking, lumbering
New York (1624)	Duke of York	Farming (cattle, rice, indigo, wheat), ironworks, shipbuilding
Pennsylvania (1682)	William Penn and *sylvania* (Latin for *forest*)	Farming (corn, wheat, cattle, dairy), papermaking, textiles, shipbuilding

 EMC 3709 · Colonial America · ©2003 by Evan-Moor Corp.

THE SOUTHERN COLONIES

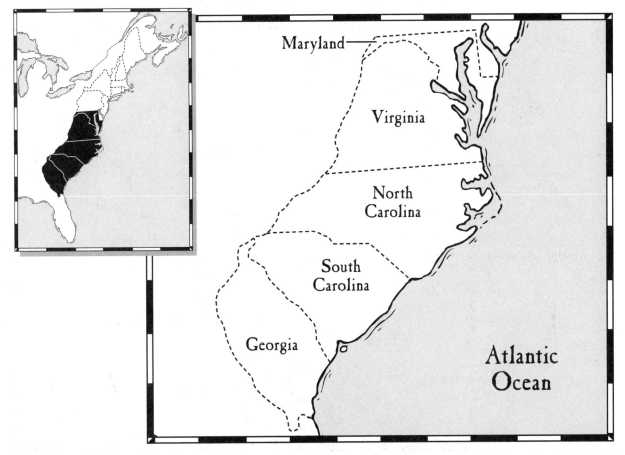

Colony (Year Founded)	Origin of Name	Chief Products
Carolina (1663) North Carolina (1712) South Carolina (1712)	Carolus (Latin for *Charles*), Charles I of England	Farming (indigo, rice, tobacco)
Georgia (1732)	King George II of England	Farming (indigo, rice, sugar)
Maryland (1632)	Queen Henrietta Maria of England	Farming (corn, indigo, rice, wheat), ironworks, shipbuilding
Virginia (1607)	Elizabeth I of England	Farming (corn, tobacco, wheat)

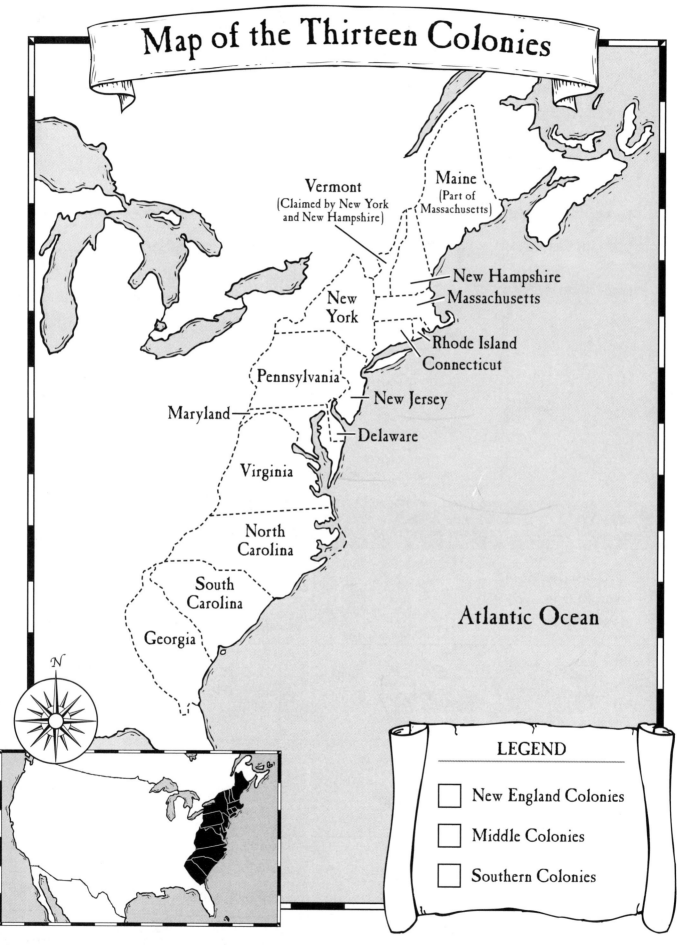

Map of the Thirteen Colonies

Vermont
(Claimed by New York
and New Hampshire)

Maine
(Part of
Massachusetts)

New Hampshire
Massachusetts

New
York

Rhode Island
Connecticut

Pennsylvania

New Jersey

Maryland

Delaware

Virginia

North
Carolina

South
Carolina

Georgia

Atlantic Ocean

N

LEGEND

New England Colonies

Middle Colonies

Southern Colonies

EMC 3709 · Colonial America · ©2003 by Evan-Moor Corp.

SETTLING THE COLONIES, A QUESTIONNAIRE

Now you know a little more about the settlement of the colonies. Pretend you are a new colonist. Fill out this questionnaire.

1. My name is _____ and I am _____ years old.

2. I came to this new place from the country of _____

3. I came to this new place in the year _____

4. I decided to immigrate because _____

_____

_____

5. When I was traveling across the ocean, I was excited and scared because

_____

_____

6. When I first came to this new place, I settled in the colony of _____

_____

7. Now I live in one of the thirteen original colonies called_____

8. I found a job as a _____

9. Here are two problems or hardships I have encountered here in this new colony:

_____

_____

10. But, here are two things I like about living in this new colony:

_____

_____

Name: _____

THE THIRTEEN COLONIES
WORD SEARCH

```
P O N M A S S A C H U S E T T S
E K E C H T H S O U N N G E O R
N R W D E L A W A R E E P U M T
N D W B C Q C U B V W W T V A U
S N E W J E R S E Y B H B I S C
Y A B Z E D G H K Z C A W R S I
L L A F I V L R C A I M U G P T
V S D E D Y O L R K J P Y I N C
A I N E W Y B O R Z U S L N Q E
N E T R W A L O N E G H K I H N
I D C E Y I A H E R G I Z A R N
A O N D N M N P A W O R N A T O
N H M A R Y L A N D N E W R U C
Y R A A N I L O R A C H T R O N
G E O R G I A T N E W N O R T H
G Y N E W M A S S V A N U C X J
```

Words to Find

Connecticut	New Hampshire	Rhode Island
Delaware	New Jersey	South Carolina
Georgia	New York	Virginia
Maryland	North Carolina	
Massachusetts	Pennsylvania	

EMC 3709 · Colonial America · ©2003 by Evan-Moor Corp.

Pocket 2

THE FIRST SETTLEMENTS

FAST FACTS

The First Settlements . . . . **page 16**
Make the bookmark about the first settlements in
colonial America, following the directions on page 2.
Students read and share interesting facts about these
settlements. Use the Fast Facts bookmark for a quick
review during transition times throughout the day.

ABOUT

The First Settlements . . . . **page 17**
Reproduce this page for students. Read and discuss
the important information to remember. Incorporate
library and multimedia resources that are available.

ACTIVITIES

The Lost Colony . . . . **page 18**
Students guess what happened to the Lost Colony of
Roanoke Island and write a short newspaper article
about it.

Map of Jamestown . . . . **pages 19 & 20**
Reproduce these pages for students. Have students
follow the directions to re-create a map of the
Jamestown fort. Provide 12" x 18" (30.5 x 45.5 cm)
construction paper for students to compile a booklet,
following the directions on page 19.

On the *Mayflower* . . . . **pages 21–23**
Life aboard the *Mayflower* was difficult. Students learn
about the conditions on the ship as they put together
a booklet about the *Mayflower*.

The Mayflower Compact . . . . **page 24**
Reproduce this page for students. After reading
about the compact the Pilgrim leaders wrote,
students are to rewrite it in their own words on
the scroll. Have students cut out the compact and
mount it on 9" x 12" (23 x 30.5 cm) black construction
paper, cutting around the edges to make a border.
Encourage students to have at least four classmates
sign their compact in ink.

THE FIRST SETTLEMENTS

©2003 by Evan-Moor Corp. • EMC 3709

THE **FIRST SETTLEMENTS**
FAST FACTS

- One theory about why the Lost Colony disappeared is that Native American groups in the area may have attacked the colonists.

- The second theory about the disappearance of the colonists at Roanoke Island is that they may have moved to the Chesapeake Bay area.

- The third theory for the disappearance of the colonists was that disease or starvation may have struck the settlement.

- Records show that Virginia Dare was the first English baby born in America. She was born on August 18, 1587, and was a member of the Lost Colony of Roanoke Island.

- For the past 200 years, historians thought the Jamestown fort was washed into the river. However, since the early 1990s, parts of the old fort have been found.

- The winter of 1609 to 1610 was called the "starving time" for the Jamestown settlers. They suffered food shortages, and many people died from dysentery and typhoid fever.

- The Pilgrims moved the cannon from the *Mayflower* and placed it on the top of a steep hill above their new village.

- The Pilgrims rebuilt an old Indian trail into a road from Plymouth to Boston.

©2003 by Evan-Moor Corp. • EMC 3709

    EMC 3709 · Colonial America · ©2003 by Evan-Moor Corp.

ABOUT
THE FIRST SETTLEMENTS

England attempted to settle colonies in America as early as the 1500s. John White led a group of colonists to settle near the Chesapeake Bay. The small group of about 120 people was forced to land on Roanoke Island instead. The island was harsh, and White returned to England for supplies. It took him three years to return to Roanoke Island. When he landed, White discovered that all the colonists had disappeared. This settlement became known as the Lost Colony.

Jamestown and Plymouth were the first two permanent English settlements in North America. They were the start of Virginia and Massachusetts, the first two of the original thirteen colonies.

In 1607 settlers arrived in Jamestown, in Chesapeake Bay. Many were wealthy and only planned to stay long enough to find gold. In 1620 Pilgrims arrived in Plymouth, near Cape Cod, seeking freedom to worship.

The Virginians came with a royal charter, meaning they had the permission of the British king to colonize. The Pilgrims had no official charter. Jamestown colonists named their settlement for England's King James I. Plymouth colonists named theirs for a port in England. They did not want to honor any British monarch!

The first Jamestown settlers were all male. Pilgrims were male and female. Neither of these groups knew how to farm or hunt. They both learned from the nearby Native Americans.

Both Jamestown and Plymouth suffered greatly in their first few years in North America. Winters were brutal and many settlers died.

In 1612 Jamestown colonists began growing tobacco. They sold a lot of it and prospered. In 1619 the first Africans arrived in Virginia as indentured servants. Soon Virginian tobacco growers stopped using indentured servants and began using African slaves.

Plymouth also grew. In 1630 many more Puritans came to the Massachusetts Bay. Boston was founded that year. Massachusetts settlers began settlements nearby in Connecticut, Rhode Island, and New Hampshire.

These early settlers made some mistakes. However, they were all very brave to move thousands of miles and try to make a life in the New World.

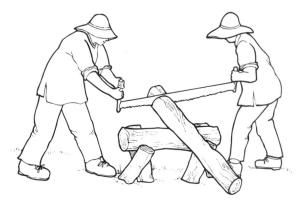

©2003 by Evan-Moor Corp. • EMC 3709 • Colonial America

Name: _____

THE LOST COLONY

In July 1587 a group of 117 men, women, and children set sail from England to the New World. Their ship was blown off course, and they landed on Roanoke Island. They faced very difficult living conditions. Supplies were used up quickly. Their leader, John White, sailed back to England for more supplies. When he returned in 1590, all the settlers had disappeared. The only clues to their whereabouts were the word CROATOAN carved on a post and CRO on a tree. White went to Croatoan Island nearby, but no one was there. White sailed back to England feeling defeated. To this day, no one knows for sure what happened to the Lost Colony at Roanoke Island. What do you think happened to the English settlers?

THE COLONIAL TIMES

_____
Headline

What Happened?

_____

_____

_____

_____

_____

_____

_____

_____   _____

_____   _____

EMC 3709 · Colonial America · ©2003 by Evan-Moor Corp.

Name: _____

MAP OF JAMESTOWN

How to Make the Map

Follow the directions below to add buildings to the map of Jamestown. Use the map legend as a guide for drawing the buildings.

1. Draw and color the **church** in the center of the fort. From 1607 until the 1750s, Jamestown went through five churches.

2. Draw and color the **marketplace** located directly in front (southwest) of the church. The marketplace was where people met to trade goods and to learn about news.

3. Draw and color the **armory** northwest of the marketplace. The armory stored the weapons for the fort. Weapons included halberds (axes), pikes (spears), muskets, and some armor.

4. Draw and color the **guardhouse** northwest of the armory near the palisade. The guardhouse was where the guards stayed and protected the fort.

5. Draw and label the **storehouse** southeast of the marketplace. The storehouse contained the colonists' most important belongings and the food for the fort.

6. Draw and color the **bunkhouses** on all three sides of the fort close to the fence lines. Historians think 20 bunkhouses were built. They were small, one-room houses shared by six to eight men. There were no women or children when the fort was first built.

7. Draw and color a cannon on each of the **bulwarks** located on the three corners of the fort. Bulwarks were the raised areas where cannons were placed.

8. Draw and color the main **gate** to the fort on the southwest palisade. Two smaller gates were located on the west and south parts of the palisade. A third smaller gate was located on the east part of the palisade.

How to Make the Booklet

Now follow these directions to make a Jamestown booklet.

1. Cut out the Jamestown map, map legend, and information on page 20.

2. Fold your construction paper in half.

3. Place the map near the fold as shown. Draw around the map, leaving a border.

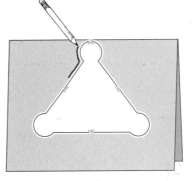

4. Cut the construction paper. Do not cut the fold.

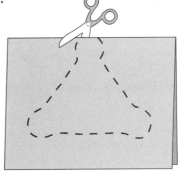

5. Glue the map and map legend on the inside of the booklet.

6. Glue the information on the front. Write a title.

©2003 by Evan-Moor Corp. • EMC 3709 • Colonial America

MAP OF JAMESTOWN

In 1607 Jamestown became the first English settlement in North America. The colonists built a fort near the James River in present-day Virginia. Walls, called palisades, surrounded the fort on all three sides.

New excavations of the area will help historians learn more about Jamestown. Archeologists have uncovered parts of the fort walls, the east cannon bulwark, a building, and more than 150,000 objects dating from 1607 to 1610.

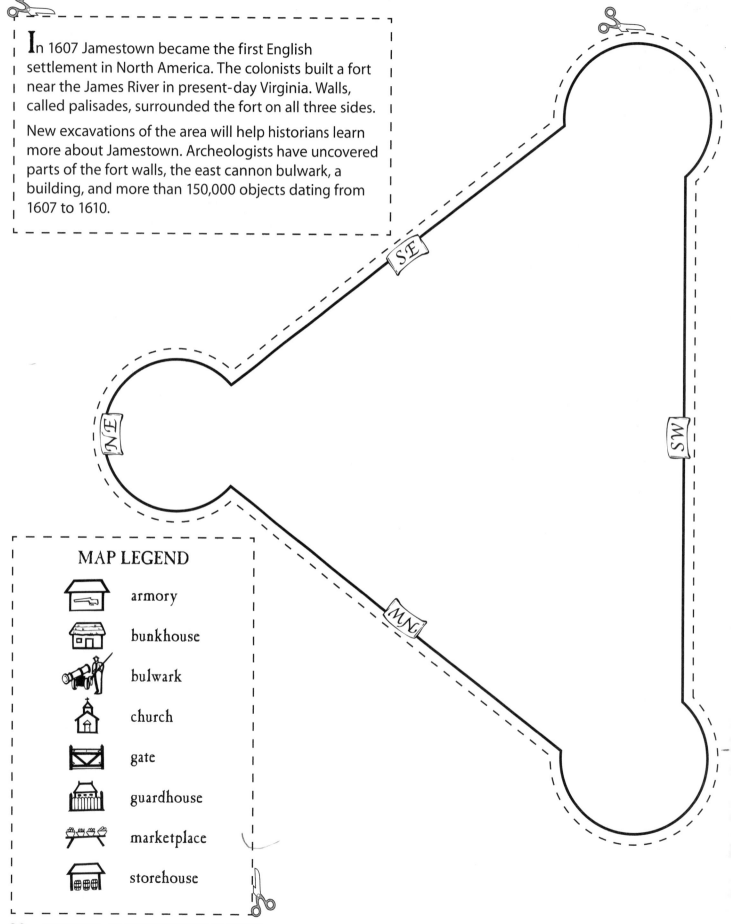

MAP LEGEND

- armory
- bunkhouse
- bulwark
- church
- gate
- guardhouse
- marketplace
- storehouse

EMC 3709 · Colonial America · ©2003 by Evan-Moor Corp.

ON THE *MAYFLOWER*

Students learn about conditions on the *Mayflower* as they reconstruct the famous ship. They also pretend they are one of the passengers and write a journal entry, telling about life on board.

STEPS TO FOLLOW

1. Read and discuss the conditions on the *Mayflower* with students.

2. Students use the hull shape to write a journal entry for one day in the life of a young person on the ship. You may choose to reproduce more copies of the journal if you want students to write entries for more than one day.

3. Have students cut out the *Mayflower* shape and mount it onto blue construction paper.

4. Direct students to cut out the journal and information in the hull shapes.

5. Have students use one of the hull shapes as a template to make a cover out of white construction paper. They write "The Mayflower" on the cover.

6. Staple the three hulls (facts, journal, and then cover) over the cutaway hull on the mounted *Mayflower* pattern.

7. Encourage students to decorate the ship using crayons and craft materials that are available.

8. Have students share their journal entries with the class.

MATERIALS

- pages 22 and 23, reproduced for each student
- 9" x 12" (23 x 30.5 cm) blue construction paper
- 6" x 12" (15 x 30.5 cm) white construction paper
- crayons or marking pens
- scissors
- glue
- stapler
- Optional: craft supplies (white tissue paper or construction paper scraps, toothpicks or craft sticks)

ON THE *MAYFLOWER*

EMC 3709 · Colonial America · ©2003 by Evan-Moor Corp.

ON THE *MAYFLOWER*

staple

staple

The voyage of the *Mayflower* from Europe to North America lasted 66 days, from September to November 1620. Each family could bring only one chest with all their belongings. Conditions on board were only tolerable. People slept squeezed between other passengers on a hard wooden deck below the main deck. Food consisted of salted meat, hardtack (dry biscuit), and limited water. Storms battered the ship, making passengers seasick and miserable. Passengers shared their quarters with cockroaches, flies, and rats. Still they maintained hope for a new life.

staple

staple

_____

_____

_____

_____

_____

©2003 by Evan-Moor Corp. • EMC 3709 • Colonial America

Name: _____

THE MAYFLOWER COMPACT

In November 1620, the Pilgrims landed on what is now the Cape Cod peninsula in Massachusetts. The Pilgrims had to make an important decision. They had to decide if they wanted to sail down the coast to Virginia, since that was their original destination, or stay up north and build a new settlement. The Pilgrims decided to stay. The leaders on board the ship demanded that every adult male sign an agreement. Women and male servants were not allowed to sign the agreement. The Mayflower Compact stated that everyone would obey an elected governor and stay together to start a new settlement. The Pilgrims agreed that they all needed to work together to survive in their new settlement.

We, the Pilgrims of Plymouth, promise

_____

_____

_____

_____

_____

_____

Signed

_____   _____

_____   _____

_____   _____

 EMC 3709 · Colonial America · ©2003 by Evan-Moor Corp.

THE NATIVE AMERICANS

FAST FACTS

The Native Americans...................... **page 26**
Make the bookmark about the Native Americans,
following the directions on page 2. Read the
interesting facts about the Native Americans. Use
the Fast Facts bookmark for a quick review during
transition times throughout the day.

ABOUT

The Native Americans...................... **page 27**
Reproduce this page for students. Read and discuss
the important information to remember. Incorporate
library and multimedia resources that are available.

ACTIVITIES

**The Legend of
"The Three Sisters"** .... **pages 28 & 29**
The Native Americans depended on three
vegetables—corn, beans, and squash. The Iroquois
even told a legend about them called "The Three
Sisters." Students create a "corn" booklet and then
become storytellers when they retell the legend of
"The Three Sisters."

Native American Words.............. **pages 30 & 31**
Many words we use today were borrowed from
Native American languages, particularly words for
food and animals the Europeans had not seen before
coming to North America. Students make a folding
mini-dictionary of their choice of Indian-influenced
words.

A Peace Treaty....................... **pages 32 & 33**
For a while, the pen was mightier than the sword
in colonial America. The first peace treaty between
settlers and Indians lasted over 50 years. Students
rewrite the terms of the peace treaty between the
Pilgrims and the Wampanoag tribe.

©2003 by Evan-Moor Corp. • EMC 3709 • Colonial America

POCKET 3 · THE NATIVE AMERICANS   **25**

THE NATIVE AMERICANS

THE NATIVE AMERICANS

FAST FACTS

- There were over 300 Native American nations, speaking 143 different languages and 1,000 dialects, living in North America when the colonists arrived.

- The Powhatan were an Algonquian-speaking group who were the first Native Americans to live side by side with English colonists in the settlement of Jamestown.

- The Native Americans traded deerskin and beaver pelts in return for metal products and textiles made by the colonists.

- European explorers, fur traders, and colonists of the 1600s learned how to make the white-birch bark canoes from the Native Americans in the northeast.

- Some Native American groups used war paint when fighting. The warriors painted their bodies with bear fat that had red coloring mixed in with it. When the Europeans saw the decorated warriors, they called them "red men."

- The Iroquois League of Nations formed a powerful, united Great Council. Benjamin Franklin observed a council meeting to learn from their form of government.

- A smallpox epidemic nearly wiped out the Native Americans who lived along the New England coast.

©2003 by Evan-Moor Corp. • EMC 3709

©2003 by Evan-Moor Corp. • EMC 3709

ABOUT
THE NATIVE AMERICANS

To Europeans, North America was the "New World." To the Native Americans, it had been home for centuries. The two worlds of the Europeans and the Native Americans met when the explorers, and then the settlers, came to North America.

An estimated 10 million Native Americans lived throughout North America when Europeans began settling there. They lived in many different confederations, or tribes. They had different languages, customs, and territories.

Algonquian-speaking groups such as the Massachuset and Wampanoag tribes lived in the northern colonial region. The Algonquin people were farmers. They grew corn, beans, and squash. Many Native Americans in this region taught European settlers how to hunt, fish, and farm.

The middle colonial region near the coast was home to such groups as the Delaware and the Iroquois. They initially welcomed settlers. They helped the first settlers hunt, fish, and build shelters. The Iroquois nation that lived inland was divided into the Cayuga, Mohawk, Oneida, Onondaga, and Seneca tribes. These tribes united to form the League of Five Nations.

The lands that made up the southern colonial region were home to tribes such as the Cherokee, the Creek, and the Powhatan. The Cherokee lived in the Carolinas, and the Creek lived in the area of present-day Georgia. The Powhatan lived by the coast of Virginia and Maryland. All these groups were excellent farmers and hunters.

When Europeans first set up communities near the Native Americans in the New World, neither group knew what to expect. Native American tribes helped the new settlers learn how to hunt, fish, and to farm the land. Sometimes the two groups fought, much of the time over land. The settlers had invaded environments that the Native Americans had lived in for hundreds of years. Native Americans did not believe humans could own land, but Europeans did.

Ultimately, Native American populations dropped significantly during this period in history, as English settlements grew and diseases brought from Europe killed numerous native peoples. The impact of European settlement during the colonial period was devastating to the Native Americans.

©2003 by Evan-Moor Corp. • EMC 3709 • Colonial America

THE
LEGEND OF
"THE THREE
SISTERS"

The Iroquois believed that
the spirits of three beautiful
sisters lived in the fields and
protected these three crops. They
wore special cornhusk masks as they
blessed the earth and asked the spirit
world to grant them a good harvest.
There are many versions of the legend of
"The Three Sisters." This is one of them.

Once there were three sisters. They were
only happy when they were together. They
were the happiest when they were planted
in the same field. The oldest sister's name was
Corn. She was tall and proud. Her slender body
and long green hair swayed in the wind. The
middle sister was called Bean. She was wiry and
graceful. Bean loved to wrap her arms around
her oldest sister, Corn. The youngest sister was
named Squash. She was shy and liked to protect
Corn and Bean. That's why she crawled along at
the feet of her two sisters.

The sisters enjoyed the warm sunshine and
[...] greatly upon the earth. Whenever one
[...] sisters grew, the other two would grow
[...] thing magical would happen to the
[...] ar summer nights. When the
[...] upon them, the three sisters
[...] ung girls. Dressed all in
[...] nd danced. They sang
[...] th and Father Sun.
[...] e fields, and the
[...] to the native
[...] Some
[...] eld on
[...] elly

MATERIALS

- page 29, reproduced for each student
- 4½" x 12" (11.5 x 30.5 cm) yellow construction paper
- 9" x 12" (23 x 30.5 cm) green construction paper
- marking pens
- scissors
- glue
- paper fastener
- hole punch

THE LEGEND OF "THE THREE SISTERS"

Students create a "corn" booklet about the Iroquois legend called "The Three Sisters."

STEPS TO FOLLOW

1. Read and discuss with students the legend of "The Three Sisters" from page 29. Remind them that storytelling was an important part of Native American life.

2. Have students cut out the "The Three Sisters" text from page 29. Direct students to glue the legend to yellow construction paper and cut around the corncob shape.

3. Instruct students to cut out two husks from green construction paper, using the husk template on page 29.

4. Have students punch a hole at the bottom of the three shapes and attach them with a paper fastener. Encourage students to add details to the "corn" booklet using marking pens.

5. Have students retell the legend to partners or to the whole class.

6. You may also want students to research other versions of the legend of "The Three Sisters."

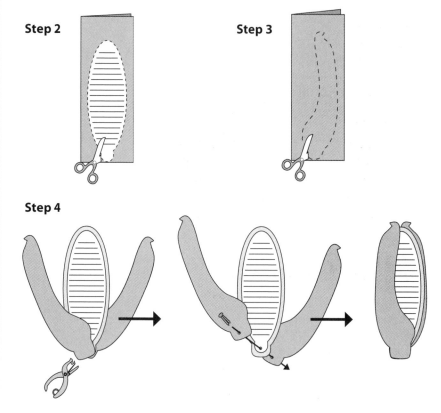

Step 2

Step 3

Step 4

EMC 3709 · Colonial America · ©2003 by Evan-Moor Corp.

CORN BOOKLET PATTERNS

THE LEGEND OF "THE THREE SISTERS"

The Iroquois believed that the spirits of three beautiful sisters lived in the fields and protected three crops. The Iroquois wore special cornhusk masks as they blessed the earth and asked the spirit world to grant them a good harvest. There are many versions of the legend of "The Three Sisters." This is one of them:

Once there were three sisters. They were only happy when they were together. They were the happiest when they were planted in the same field. The oldest sister's name was Corn. She was tall and proud. Her slender body and long green hair swayed in the wind. The middle sister was called Bean. She was wiry and graceful. Bean loved to wrap her arms around her oldest sister, Corn. The youngest sister was named Squash. She was shy and liked to protect Corn and Bean. That's why she crawled along at the feet of her two sisters.

The sisters enjoyed the warm sunshine and smiled greatly upon the earth. Whenever one of the sisters grew, the other two would grow too. Something magical would happen to the sisters on clear summer nights. When the moon shined upon them, the three sisters changed into young girls. Dressed all in green, they sang and danced. They sang praises to Mother Earth and Father Sun.

Harvest time came to the fields, and the sisters gave nourishment to the native peoples living in the region. Some say if you go out into a cornfield on a moonlit night, you can actually hear the crops growing. The three sisters are once again protecting a new crop of corn, beans, and squash.

NATIVE AMERICAN WORDS

Rich language is among the many contributions that Native people made to American culture. Students create a folding mini-dictionary of Native American words in common use today.

MATERIALS

- page 31, reproduced for each student
- 8" x 36" (20 x 91 cm) piece of sturdy paper (butcher paper, shelf paper, or brown wrapping paper)
- ruler
- pencil
- crayons or marking pens
- scissors
- hole punch
- 1 yard (1 m) of yarn, string, or narrow ribbon

STEPS TO FOLLOW

1. Discuss the fact that many English words come from Native American languages.

2. Measure to divide the book into six pages. Each page will be 6" (15 cm) wide. Mark the pages at 6" (15 cm), 12" (30.5 cm), 18" (45.5 cm), 24" (61 cm), and 30" (76 cm). Mark along both the top and bottom of the paper.

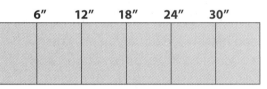

3. Carefully fold at each mark. Fold the paper like an accordion. Fold the first page to the right and the second to the left. The folding pattern is right, left, right, left, right.

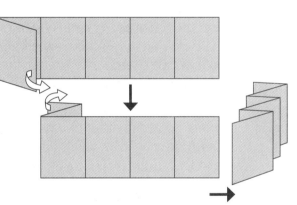

4. Students follow the directions on page 31 to make a mini-dictionary featuring 11 Native American words. Students may need to use an adult dictionary to get the definition of some of the words.

5. Then students use the hole punch to make two holes in the center (near the outside edge) of the first and the last pages.

6. Thread a piece of yarn through the holes on the first page. The loose ends of the yarn will hang down the first page. Gently wrap the yarn around the book and through the two holes on the back page. Thread the yarn through the front holes again and tie a bow.

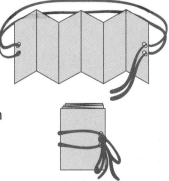

7. Have students put a title and picture on the front cover.

EMC 3709 · Colonial America · ©2003 by Evan-Moor Corp.

Name: _____

MINI-DICTIONARY OF NATIVE AMERICAN WORDS

Choose 11 of the following words to put in the mini-dictionary that you have made. Look up each word in the dictionary. On each page of your mini-dictionary:

- Write the English word.
- Write the Native American language group the word originated from.
- Write the definition of the word.
- Add a colored illustration for the word.

When you are finished, add a decorative cover for your mini-dictionary.

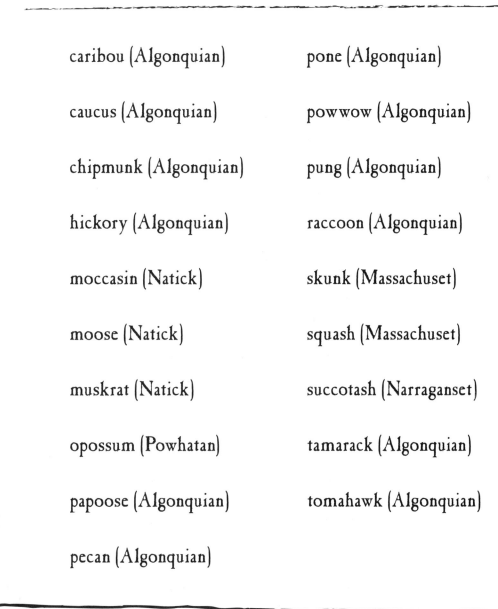

caribou (Algonquian)   pone (Algonquian)

caucus (Algonquian)   powwow (Algonquian)

chipmunk (Algonquian)   pung (Algonquian)

hickory (Algonquian)   raccoon (Algonquian)

moccasin (Natick)   skunk (Massachuset)

moose (Natick)   squash (Massachuset)

muskrat (Natick)   succotash (Narraganset)

opossum (Powhatan)   tamarack (Algonquian)

papoose (Algonquian)   tomahawk (Algonquian)

pecan (Algonquian)

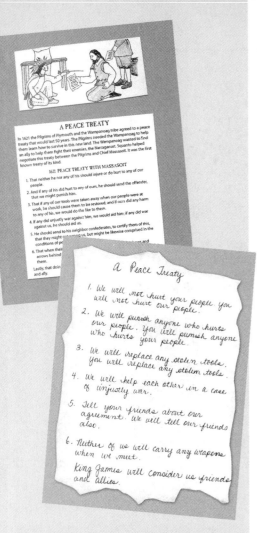

A PEACE TREATY

Students are given the terms of the treaty between the Pilgrims and the Wampanoag tribe. They interpret the words and then rewrite the terms of a treaty in their own words.

STEPS TO FOLLOW

1. Discuss the differences the Europeans and the Native Americans might have had that required a peace treaty.

2. Distribute page 33. Read the background information and the six points of the treaty as a class. Explain the archaic language and clarify meanings.

3. On writing paper, have students rewrite the six points in their own words and sign the document. Encourage them to write in cursive and use ink.

4. Students cut out and glue the information and picture to one side of the construction paper and glue the writing paper to the other side . Have students carefully tear the edges of the construction paper to make the treaty look tattered and worn.

5. Have students share their interpretations of the treaty with the whole class.

MATERIALS

- page 33, reproduced for each student
- 9" x 12" (23 x 30.5 cm) brown or tan construction paper
- writing paper
- pen
- scissors
- glue

A PEACE TREATY

In 1621 the Pilgrims of Plymouth and the Wampanoag tribe agreed to a peace treaty that would last 50 years. The Pilgrims needed the Wampanoag to help them learn how to survive in this new land. The Wampanoag wanted to find an ally to help them fight their enemies, the Narraganset. Squanto helped negotiate this treaty between the Pilgrims and Chief Massasoit. It was the first known treaty of its kind.

1621 PEACE TREATY WITH MASSASOIT

1. That neither he nor any of his should injure or do hurt to any of our people.

2. And if any of his did hurt to any of ours, he should send the offender, that we might punish him.

3. That if any of our tools were taken away when our people were at work, he should cause them to be restored; and if ours did any harm to any of his, we would do the like to them.

4. If any did unjustly war against him, we would aid him; if any did war against us, he should aid us.

5. He should send to his neighbor confederates, to certify them of this, that they might not wrong us, but might be likewise comprised in the conditions of peace.

6. That when their men came to us, they should leave their bows and arrows behind them, as we should do our pieces when we came to them.

Lastly, that doing thus, King James would esteem of him as his friend and ally.

HOMES AND VILLAGES

FAST FACTS

Make the bookmark about homes and villages,
following the directions on page 2. Students read and
share the interesting facts about homes and villages.
Use the Fast Facts bookmark for a quick review during
transition times throughout the day.

ABOUT

Reproduce this page for students. Read and discuss
the information to remember. Incorporate library and
multimedia resources that are available.

ACTIVITIES

Students experience how cramped early colonists
must have felt living in a one-room house. They make
a colonial home and add the sparse furnishings to it.

Reproduce these pages for students. Students follow
the directions to make a map of a typical colonial
village.

Reproduce these pages for students. Students
follow the directions to match the descriptions of
the buildings found on a southern plantation to the
pictures. Provide each student with scissors, glue,
and a 12" x 18" (30.5 x 45.5 cm) piece of construction
paper.

EMC 3709 · Colonial America · ©2003 by Evan-Moor Corp.

©2003 by Evan-Moor Corp. • EMC 3709

HOMES AND VILLAGES

FAST FACTS

- In New England, house-raisings were popular. A group of men and boys built an entire house in one day. Meanwhile, the women and girls prepared a huge meal for the workers.

- Glass windows were extremely rare and expensive. If a family left their home for a long period, they removed the glass panes and took them along on the trip.

- It was common for wooden homes to burn down every few years. The precious iron nails were retrieved from the ashes, and the owner would start building a new home.

- Wealthy southern plantation owners had their homes built out of expensive brick rather than wood.

- Early colonial homes did not have bathrooms. Colonists used outhouses some distance from the house. In winter they used chamber pots that had to be emptied daily.

- In the 1600s the Swedish colonists who settled in Delaware built the first log cabins in America. By the 1700s log cabins became the most popular type of home with the pioneers heading west.

- In the center of the village was an open area called the village green, or the common. This was where cattle grazed, children played, and colonists gathered to hear the most recent news.

©2003 by Evan-Moor Corp. • EMC 3709

ABOUT
HOMES AND VILLAGES

When the first colonists arrived in the New World, they had to find or make temporary shelters until permanent homes could be built. They made tents, lived in caves, or even stayed aboard the ship while they built their homes and villages. Each section of the colonies developed its own style of houses, depending on the climate and the natural resources available.

In the New England colonies, simple wood-plank houses were built. The roofs were either thatched or had wood shingles. The house was usually one long room with a large fireplace at one end. The room was a kitchen, bedroom, and living room all in one. The house had dirt floors, and small windows kept it dark even in the daytime. The beams supported a loft, where supplies were stored.

In the middle colonies, many colonists built log cabins because the forests provided so much wood. Tables, chairs, and stools were all made of log slabs held together with wooden pegs. The Dutch introduced another type of fancier home in the middle colonies. The houses were one-and-a-half stories high and had a small porch in front. The front door was divided into halves that opened separately. Another unique feature was that the beds were hidden in walls and opened like cupboards.

The majority of people living in the southern colonies lived in small wooden houses with wood shingles. However, what most people remember about the southern colonies is the plantation mansion. A typical plantation home was two-stories high and had eight rooms. The main house had imported furniture and carpets. The kitchen, laundry, and other buildings stood nearby. There were also small, one-room houses for the servants and slaves. Each plantation was run like an independent village. There were shops, offices, and a school. However, unlike villages in other parts of the colonies, these cotton and tobacco plantations used forced slave labor.

Colonists up and down the eastern seaboard cleared more and more land to build their villages. As time went on, these small villages grew into towns. By the 1700s towns grew into cities such as Boston, Philadelphia, Providence, and Williamsburg.

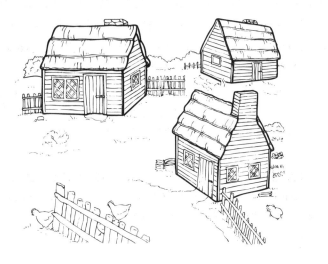

   EMC 3709 · Colonial America · ©2003 by Evan-Moor Corp.

AN EARLY COLONIAL HOME

Early New England homes consisted of one room that served as the living room, kitchen, and bedroom for the whole family. Students experience that cramped space as they make a colonial home, complete with the sparse furnishings.

STEPS TO FOLLOW

1. To make the home, guide students through the following steps:

   a. Fold construction paper in half. Crease.

   b. Fold sides in to meet in the center. Open these folds.

   c. Fold each top corner down to meet the fold line. Crease. Fold toward the back. Crease again.

   d. Open up the paper all the way. Push in on the horizontal fold, bringing the corner folds together to create the slope of the roof.

Step 1a

Step 1b

Step 1c

Step 1d

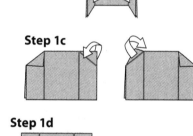
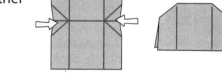

MATERIALS

- page 38, reproduced for each student
- 9" x 12" (23 x 30.5 cm) tan construction paper
- writing paper
- scissors
- glue
- crayons or marking pens
- waxed paper scraps
- transparent tape
- pencil

2. Have students color and cut out the roof on page 38. They glue it to the front of the house.

3. Direct students to cut a 3" (7.5 cm) door in the home. Cut only one side and top, and then fold back so the door will open.

4. Have students cut out two small 1" (2.5 cm) square windows. Have students tape waxed paper to the windows.

5. Direct students to color and cut out the furnishings of the colonial house. Then they arrange and glue the furnishings inside the house. Students should also draw in more details of the house.

6. Glue the writing paper on the back of the house. Have students write about what they would have liked and disliked about living in an early colonial home.

©2003 by Evan-Moor Corp. • EMC 3709 • Colonial America

EARLY COLONIAL HOME FURNISHINGS

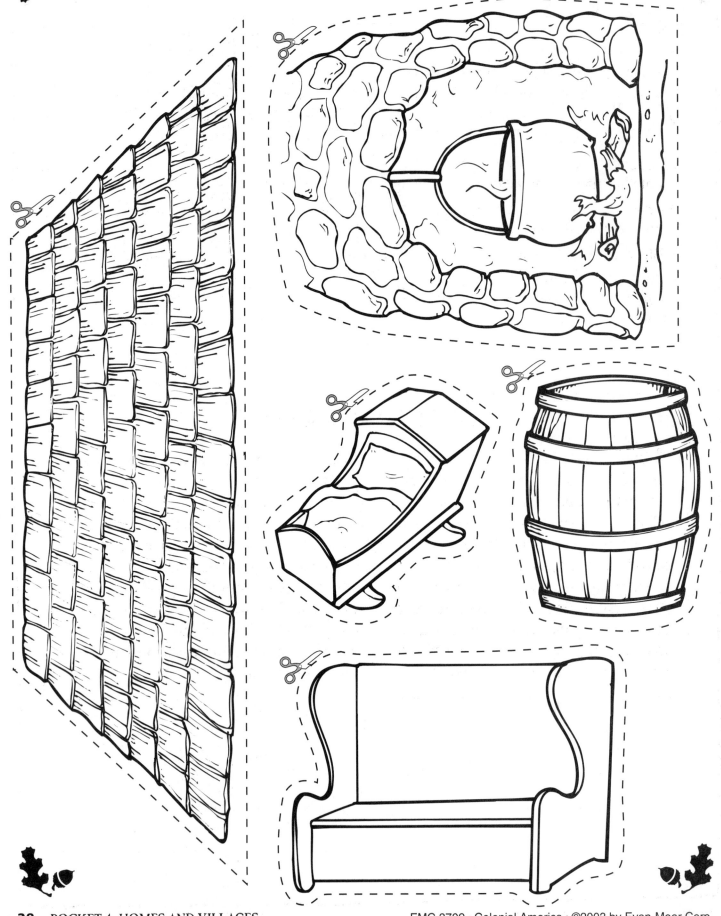

   EMC 3709 · Colonial America · ©2003 by Evan-Moor Corp.

A COLONIAL VILLAGE

DIRECTIONS

1. Cut out the village green and mount it to 9" x 12" (23 x 30.5 cm) white construction paper.

2. Read the information about a colonial village below.

3. Cut out the buildings, glue them onto the map, and label them.

4. Add other buildings and items mentioned in the information.

5. Give your village a name.

6. Cut out and glue the information about a colonial village onto the back of your map.

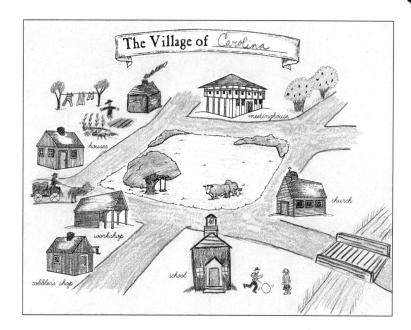

A COLONIAL VILLAGE

The village was an important unit in colonial America. Some colonists stayed in one village all their lives. A typical village started with an open area called the village green. Here cattle grazed and children played. There was a meetinghouse, a church, and a school in most villages. Each village had a general store where goods were bought and mail was exchanged. Shops lined the dirt streets. Some shopkeepers were the blacksmith; the cooper, who made barrels and buckets; the chandler, who made candles; the printer; the cobbler, to make and fix shoes; the tailor; and the furniture maker. There was usually a tavern and a cider mill on the outskirts of the village. Homes were built both in the village and on the outskirts of town. Each home had a vegetable garden and pens for the animals. Surrounding the village was farmland and a river.

A COLONIAL VILLAGE

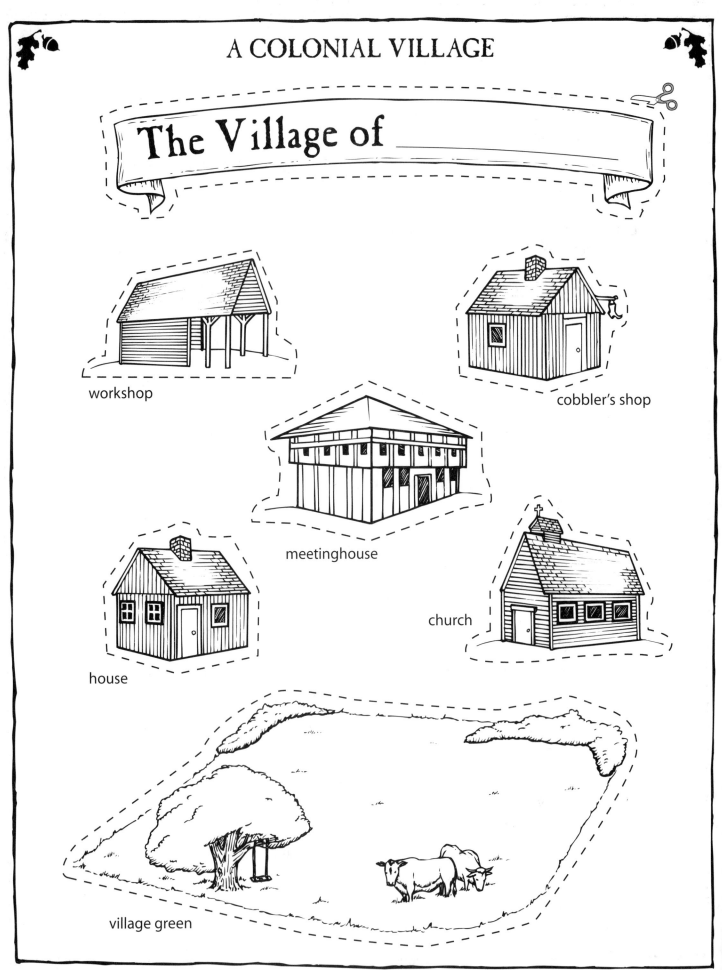

The Village of _____

workshop

cobbler's shop

meetinghouse

house

church

village green

EMC 3709 · Colonial America · ©2003 by Evan-Moor Corp.

A SOUTHERN PLANTATION

Plantations in the southern colonies were large farms that specialized in growing one valuable crop, such as tobacco or cotton. Plantations were so large that they resembled a village.

Read the numbered sentences that describe the different buildings on a southern plantation. Look at the map of the southern plantation as you read the descriptions. Write the number of each description in the circle of the building being described. Color and cut out the plantation scene. Mount the scene on construction paper. Cut out and glue the numbered sentences next to the map.

1. The planter and his family lived in the mansion called the Big House.

2. Meals for the planter's family were prepared in a kitchen, which was right next door to the Big House.

3. A smokehouse located on the other side of the Big House was used to preserve meats.

4. Next to the smokehouse was the well or springhouse, which provided water.

5. The icehouse was circular in shape and was used to preserve milk and fresh meat.

6. Laundry was done in the washhouse.

7. The carriage house stored the planter's coaches and carriages.

8. Right behind the carriage house was the shoemaker's shop.

9. The large barn and stables were for the horses, cows, sheep, and chickens.

10. In the blacksmith's shop, iron tools and horseshoes were made. This shop was located between the large barn and the carriage house.

11. The slave quarters, or groups of small houses, were built at the back of the property near the fields.

12. In the spinning house, slaves carded the wool and spun it into yarn. In the weaving house, slaves made the cloth. The cloth was made into clothing in the sewing house.

13. In the carpentry shop, wood planks, furniture, and even coffins were made.

14. A house was used to make candles and soap. Tallow, or fat, was melted in the soap kettle.

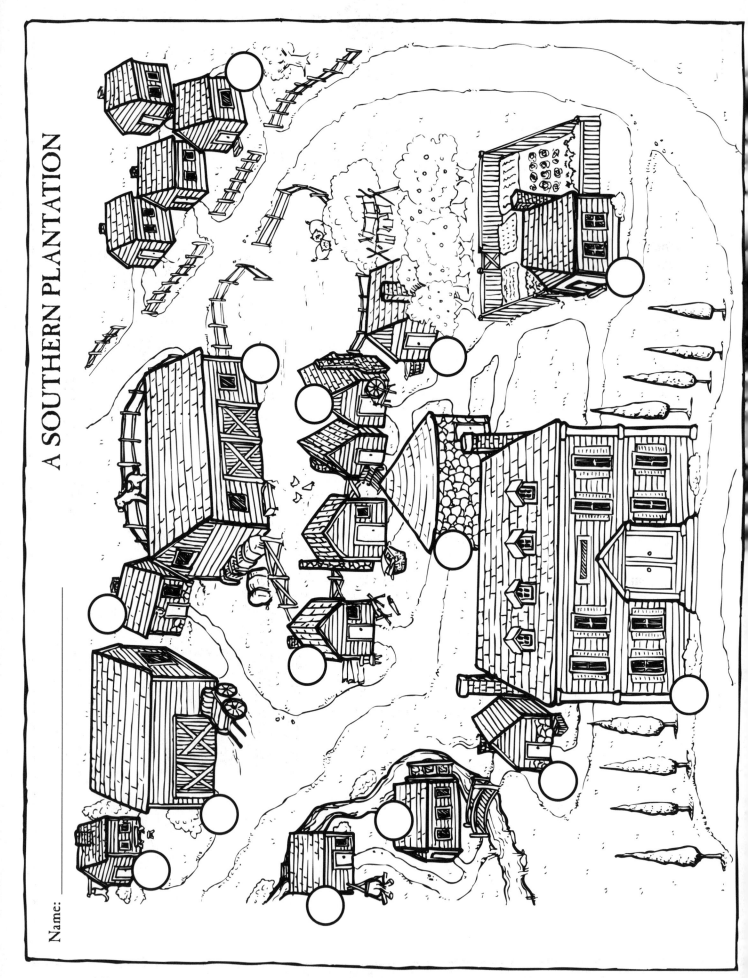

A SOUTHERN PLANTATION

Name:

EMC 3709 · Colonial America · ©2003 by Evan-Moor Corp.

Pocket 5

DAILY LIFE

FAST FACTS

Make the bookmark about daily life in colonial America, following the directions on page 2. Read the interesting facts about daily life. Use the Fast Facts bookmark for a quick review during transition times throughout the day.

ABOUT

Reproduce this page for students. Read and discuss the important information to remember. Incorporate library and multimedia resources that are available.

ACTIVITIES

Students learn about the different food that the colonists ate each season of the year. They make a collage of baskets of food for each season.

The most familiar type of clothing in colonial America is that of the Pilgrims. Students dress a man and woman in the clothing of the 1600s.

Colonial girls were expected to have a sampler, a piece of fabric showing all the sewing stitches they could do. Students will create their own samplers using graph paper instead of cloth.

Colonial children worked hard, but they did like to play. Have students make a toy called Jacob's ladder to show that they are able to tackle a challenging handmade project.

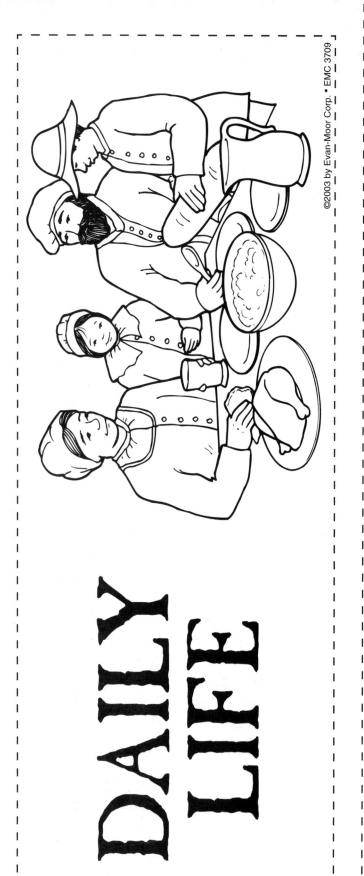

DAILY LIFE

DAILY LIFE
FAST FACTS

- The colonists' main meal of the day was eaten between noon and 3 P.M. Sounds like lunch? They called it dinner. So what did they call dinner? Supper.

- Only wealthy families could afford to eat with forks. Most families ate with their fingers.

- In Puritan families, children had to stand at the table to eat. It was considered impolite for children to talk while eating.

- To show respect, colonial children had to bow and curtsy to adults, including their parents.

- Both boys and girls in colonial New England wore dresses until they were about seven years old.

- Beginning in the late 1600s, wigs were stylish for colonial men. In the 1700s it became fashionable to cover wigs with white powder.

- Most colonists thought bathing was unhealthy and did it only a few times a year!

- Fun was mixed with work. Before a barn dance began, kernels of corn were thrown on the floor. While people danced, the feet of the dancers pressed the oil from the kernels into the raw wood, helping to make it smooth and polished.

©2003 by Evan-Moor Corp. • EMC 3709

©2003 by Evan-Moor Corp. • EMC 3709

ABOUT
DAILY LIFE

The daily life of the colonists centered around the home. Men, women, and children worked hard from early morning until late at night. Most everything in the home had to be made by hand.

Clothing

Colonial clothing varied from region to region. The style of clothing also depended on religious beliefs, social class, and occupations. Most colonists wore simple, plain clothing made of linen, wool, and leather. Roots, berries, and leaves were used as dyes for the clothes. The usual colors for the clothes were tan, brown, and a yellowish-brown or reddish-brown. Both boys and girls dressed exactly like their parents. Wealthier colonists imitated the styles of Europe. Their clothing was made from fine linen, cotton, silk, satin, and velvet.

Food

Typically colonists ate mush (porridge) in the mornings, stews at noon, and stew leftovers with bread and cheese at night. Most meals were cooked in a large iron pot. One of the most important foods was corn, prepared in a variety of ways. They also had other vegetables such as beans, squash, and sweet potatoes. Cows provided the butter and cheese, and hogs provided the bacon and ham. Wild game such as deer, pheasant, and turkey was also common. In addition to meat, the Atlantic coast provided a variety of seafood such as eels, clams, crabs, and oysters. Apples, peaches, and berries were abundant. Cider and beer were common drinks.

Recreation

Although lifestyles were hard and rules strict, colonists did like to have fun. However, the fun was usually associated with some kind of work. Quilting bees and huskings were popular. Women gathered to visit while they made quilts. Competitive cornhusking games made work more enjoyable. Music and dancing were common at weddings and other social events. Children played games such as hopscotch, leapfrog, marbles, and tag. They also enjoyed checkers and backgammon. Homemade cornhusk dolls, kites, and spinning tops were favorite toys. All colonists enjoyed fairs. Fairs provided farmers a chance to sell produce and to have fun at the same time. Participating in contests and seeing puppet shows, animal acts, and jugglers made going to the fair a fun family event.

FOOD FOR ALL SEASONS

Each season of the year colonists had a variety of foods that they ate. Students find out about the different kinds of foods when they make a seasonal collage.

STEPS TO FOLLOW

1. Discuss the different kinds of foods the colonists ate each season.

2. Have students cut out the four baskets and glue them onto construction paper. Remind students that they are going to add pictures and words to the baskets to make a collage effect.

3. Direct students to cut out pictures of seasonal foods from magazines and glue them in the appropriate baskets.

4. Encourage students to also draw pictures and add words to each basket.

5. You may choose to have students glue raffia to the baskets and add kernels of corn to the collage.

6. On the back of the collage, have students make a list of foods they like to eat. Ask them if there are particular foods they eat in each season of the year.

MATERIALS

- page 47, reproduced on brown paper for each student
- 9" x 12" (23 x 30.5 cm) construction paper
- pencil
- crayons or marking pens
- scissors
- glue
- nature and food magazines
- Optional: raffia and unpopped popcorn

EMC 3709 · Colonial America · ©2003 by Evan-Moor Corp.

FOOD FOR ALL SEASONS

SPRING

SUMMER

FALL

WINTER

Spring	Summer	Fall	Winter	Any Season
fish and seafood, nuts, blackberries, and blueberries	strawberries, corn, beans, squash, and sweet potatoes	peaches, apples, and wild game	dried fruit and wild game	ham and bacon, butter and cheese, corn bread and stews

Note: Reproduce pages 48–50 for students to use with the "Colonial Dress" activity, as described on page 43.

COLONIAL DRESS

Follow the directions to dress a colonial man and woman.

1. Read the information below about how men and women dressed in the New England colonies.

2. Cut out and glue the man to 6" x 9" (15 x 23 cm) sheet of construction paper.

3. Color the man's articles of clothing and then carefully cut out each piece. Using the information below, glue each piece of clothing on the model, layer by layer, in the correct order. Glue only at the top of each article of clothing so each layer of clothing may be seen when you flip them up.

4. Glue the information about the clothing of a colonial man on the back of the construction paper. Cut around the figure, leaving a narrow border of color. When you finish, you should have a well-dressed colonial man.

5. Follow the same directions for making the colonial woman.

COLONIAL M

COLONIAL WOMAN

Men in New England wore white linen shirts. A tightly fitting jacket called a doublet was worn over the shirt. Sometimes the men wore a ruffled collar. Long woolen stockings that came over the knees were tucked into short pants called breeches. Garters kept the stockings in place. Tall, wide-brimmed felt hats were worn both inside and outside. Shoes were made of leather.

Women in New England wore a basic undergarment much like the shirt, which was called a shift. A petticoat was worn over this. The outermost clothing was either a gown, or a fitted jacket (called a waistcoat) and skirt. A long white apron and a soft white cap, called a coif, completed the outfit. Women hung pockets on the outside of their aprons. Leather shoes were similar to the men's shoes.

EMC 3709 · Colonial America · ©2003 by Evan-Moor Corp.

COLONIAL MAN

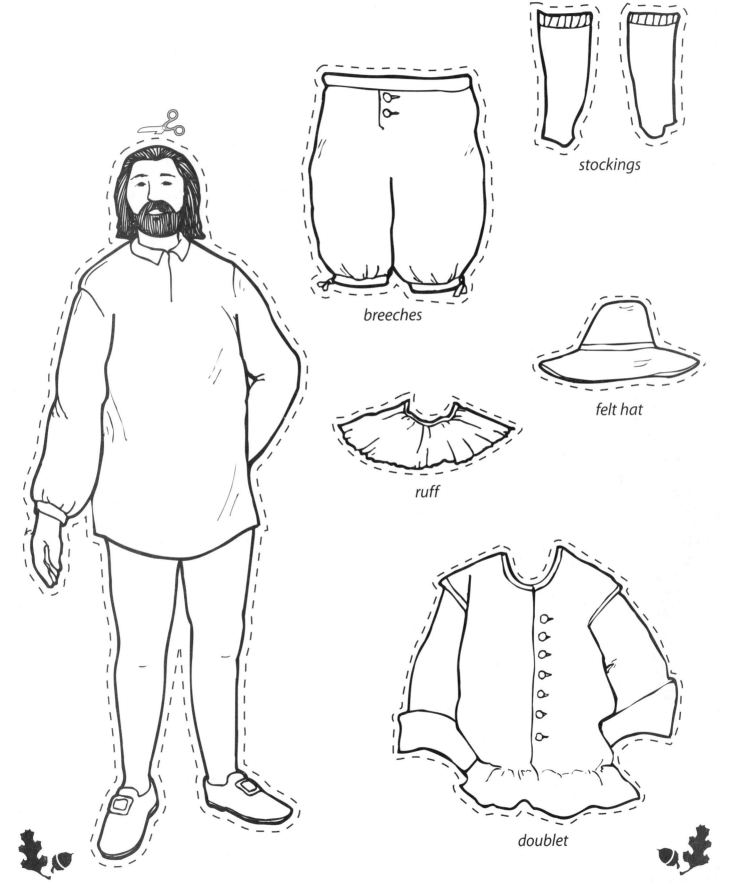

stockings

breeches

felt hat

ruff

doublet

©2003 by Evan-Moor Corp. • EMC 3709 • Colonial America

COLONIAL WOMAN

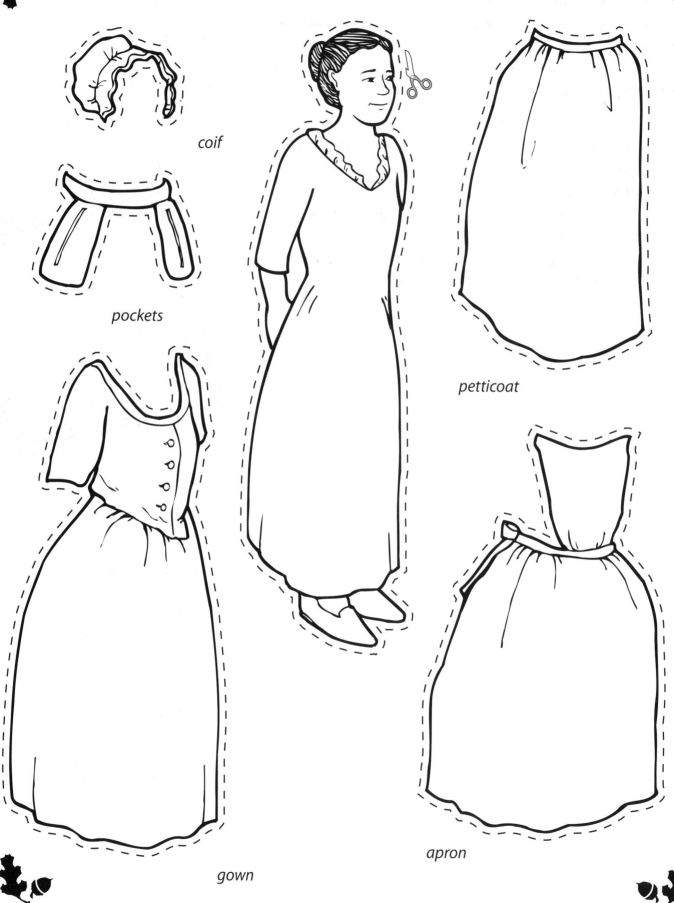

coif

pockets

petticoat

gown

apron

EMC 3709 · Colonial America · ©2003 by Evan-Moor Corp.

TRY A SAMPLE

Students learn about the craft of sewing and then create their own samplers.

STEPS TO FOLLOW

1. Have students read about the skill of sewing on page 52.

2. Direct students to study and then color the sampler design.

3. Instruct students to create two original designs of samplers on graph paper.

4. Students cut out their favorite sampler and mount it on construction paper.

5. Have students make a frame around the sampler using craft materials (ribbon, buttons, craft sticks, etc.).

MATERIALS

- page 52, reproduced for each student
- 9" x 12" (23 x 30.5 cm) construction paper
- three or four sheets of 1/4" (0.6 cm) graph paper
- pencil
- marking pens
- scissors
- glue
- craft materials: ribbon, craft sticks, buttons, etc.

©2003 by Evan-Moor Corp. • EMC 3709 • Colonial America

SAMPLER

Colonial girls spent a lot of time learning to sew. This skill was necessary because all clothes, bed linens, and tablecloths were made by hand. Girls were expected to have a sampler, a piece of fabric showing all the sewing stitches they could do. Two kinds of stitches that were used on the sampler were the running stitch and the cross-stitch. The sampler usually included the alphabet and a Bible passage. Girls knew they might be able to earn a living using their sewing skills one day.

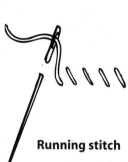

Cross-stitch

Running stitch

EMC 3709 · Colonial America · ©2003 by Evan-Moor Corp.

JACOB'S LADDER

Toys in the New England colonies were usually made from inexpensive scrap materials. Jacob's ladders were made from pieces of scrap wood and ribbons from old clothing. The toy was supposed to remind children of the Bible story of the prophet Jacob, who dreamt of a ladder that led to Heaven. During all-day church services, children were allowed to play with Jacob's ladders to help keep them quiet.

Students follow directions to make this homemade toy.

STEPS TO FOLLOW

1. Gather up all the materials for students. You may want students to work in groups so they can help each other. You may also want to make a sample of the toy to familiarize yourself with the steps of the project.

2. Discuss the background information about the Jacob's ladder toy with students.

3. Have students finely sand all sides of the four blocks of wood before they begin putting the toy together.

4. Read and look at the visual steps on how to make the toy several times with students before beginning the project.

5. Have students follow the directions on pages 54 and 55 for making the toy.

6. After the students have made the toy, show them how to play with the ladder.

7. Allow them to play with the toy. Have them pretend they are colonial children (so they may not talk while they are playing with the toy).

MATERIALS

- pages 54 and 55, reproduced for each student or group
- four equally sized blocks of wood, each 2½" to 3" (6 to 7.5 cm) square and ½" (1 cm) thick
- fine sandpaper
- three pieces of narrow ribbon, each 14" (35.5 cm) long
- scissors
- hammer
- 12 flat-head thumbtacks

©2003 by Evan-Moor Corp. • EMC 3709 • Colonial America

MAKING A JACOB'S LADDER

STEPS TO FOLLOW

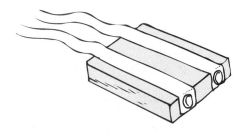

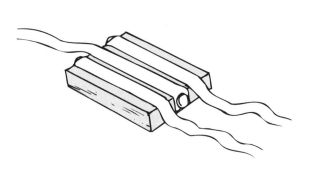

1. Using the hammer and two tacks, gently tack two of the ribbons to the end of one of the wood blocks about one fourth of the way in from each side. Lay the ribbons across the block.

2. Turn the wood block so the tacks are facing away from you and the ribbons are coming toward you. Tack the third piece of ribbon to the end of the wood block facing you between the first two ribbons. Lay that ribbon across the block and away from you.

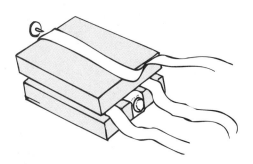

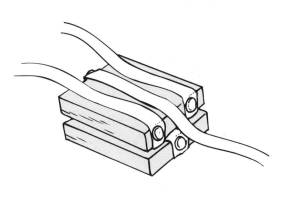

3. Place another wood block on top, with the ribbons in the middle and their tails hanging out. Tack the center ribbon on the end of the block facing away from you.

4. Pull up the other two ribbons and tack them to the end of the top block closest to you.

EMC 3709 · Colonial America · ©2003 by Evan-Moor Corp.

MAKING A JACOB'S LADDER

STEPS TO FOLLOW continued

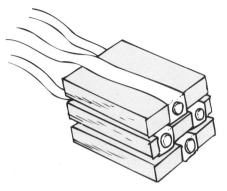

5. Put the third block on top, sandwiching all three ribbons in between blocks two and three. Pull up the middle ribbon and tack it to the end closest to you.

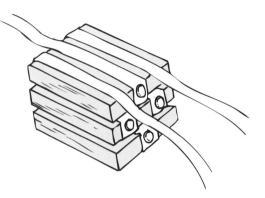

6. Pull the two outer ribbons up over the top of the block. Tack them to the end farthest from you.

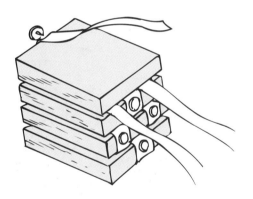

7. Place the fourth block on top. Make sure all three ribbons are between the top two blocks. Pull the middle ribbon up over the top of the block. Tack it on the end farthest from you.

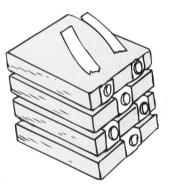

8. Pull up the two outer ribbons and tack them to the end closest to you. Trim the excess from all three ribbons.

HOW TO PLAY

Pick up the top block by its edges. Tilt the block until it touches the second block. The block will look as if it is tumbling down.

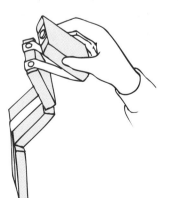

Pocket 6

SCHOOL

FAST FACTS

Make the bookmark about school in colonial America, following the directions on page 2. Student read and share interesting facts about school. Use the Fast Facts bookmark for a quick review during transition times throughout the day.

ABOUT

Reproduce this page for students. Read and discuss the important information to remember. Incorporate library and multimedia resources that are available.

ACTIVITIES

Practicing penmanship was a daily task for students in colonial America. Students experience this firsthand when they make and use a "quill" pen to write the alphabet in cursive.

Colonial children studied using hornbooks, paddle-shaped boards to which lessons were pasted. Students make a hornbook.

Children in colonial America had barely enough time in the day to play. Students compare their daily routine to the rigorous routine of children in colonial America.

EMC 3709 · Colonial America · ©2003 by Evan-Moor Corp.

SCHOOL

©2003 by Evan-Moor Corp. • EMC 3709

SCHOOL

FAST FACTS

- Boys who talked to their friends in school were given the "whispering stick." A whispering stick was a small tree branch that was placed in the boy's mouth to keep him quiet.

- It was more important for children to have perfect penmanship than to spell correctly.

- Some rich boys were sent to college in England by the time they were 11 years old.

- In 1635 the first public school in the colonies opened in Boston.

- In 1636 Harvard College was founded in the Massachusetts Bay Colony.

- By the time of the American Revolution, there were colleges in many other colonies, including William and Mary (Virginia), Yale (Connecticut), Princeton (New Jersey), Columbia (New York), and Brown (Rhode Island).

- In 1681 Pennsylvania founder William Penn said that children in his colony must learn the three Rs: "reading, 'ritin', and 'rithmetic" (reading, writing, and arithmetic).

- One rule in *The School of Good Manners* was "Stuff not thy mouth so as to fill thy Cheeks; be content with smaller Mouthfuls." Has that rule lasted to the present?

©2003 by Evan-Moor Corp. • EMC 3709

ABOUT
SCHOOL

In the earliest days of colonial America, parents taught children at home. To some families, it was more valuable for children to learn to farm rather than to read. Going to school only took able workers (the children) away from the fields! For other families, both school education and farm education were equally important.

Formal education was especially important in the New England colonies. Most Puritans were educated people, and they wanted their children to be too. Parents usually educated young boys and girls at home. Often, a woman in the village taught several young children in her home. These schools were called dame schools. The young children learned how to read and write.

When children got a little older, some children attended schools taught by men called schoolmasters. A woman who taught in a school had to quit teaching when she married. The schoolmasters were very strict, and students were punished harshly for disobedience. Students were expected to have perfect manners.

On a typical school day, children sat on long wooden benches completing lessons in math and grammar. Students studied a book called *The New England Primer,* first published in 1690, which helped children learn the alphabet with a series of short rhymes. One other book that was part of a good education was the Bible.

After a few years of basic education, formal school ended for most children. Boys learned a trade from their families or through an apprenticeship. Sons of rich families attended colleges. Girls learned household skills from their mothers. Daughters of rich families were sent off to finishing schools, where they learned music, painting, and a foreign language.

Massachusetts passed a law in 1642 that parents had to teach their children to read. Another law was passed in 1647 that towns with 50 or more families had to have a schoolteacher whose salary was paid by the town inhabitants—even those who had no children. That was the start of the public school system in America, in which every child can be educated no matter how much money the family has.

EMC 3709 · Colonial America · ©2003 by Evan-Moor Corp.

PRACTICE MAKES PERFECT

Students find out how hard it is to write when they have to use a "quill" pen to practice the alphabet in cursive.

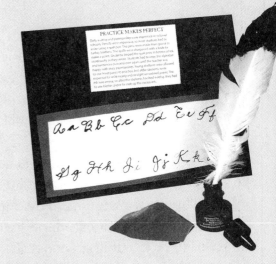

STEPS TO FOLLOW

1. Read the information on page 60 about writing in colonial schools.

2. Have students make their own "quill" pen following the directions:

   a. Look at the feather and notice the tube-like part of the feather. It is called the quill.

   quill

   b. Use a piece of sandpaper to rub one edge of the quill to make it into a sharp point.

   c. Soak the point in water for five minutes to make it softer.

   d. Cut a small notch in the point of the quill with scissors so it will hold the ink better.

3. Direct students to practice writing a cursive alphabet on lined paper or white bond paper. Have students put another piece of paper under the one they are writing on to absorb extra ink. They should dip just the tip of the quill in a bottle of liquid ink and practice writing alphabet letters. Assure students that it takes lots of practice to get it just right!

4. Remind students to allow the paper to dry completely.

5. Have students glue their writing sample onto construction paper. They may add a decorative border around their work. You may also want students to glue the information and alphabet model on the back of the construction paper for further reference.

Other hints:

- You may want to make the "quill" pens in small groups while the other students practice writing in cursive using a pen.

- Divide the ink into small trays to make it go farther.

- If supplies are limited, a similar effect may be achieved by using a calligraphy pen or a fountain pen.

MATERIALS

- page 60, reproduced for each student

- writing paper or bond paper

- 9" x 12" (23 x 30.5 cm) construction paper

- bird quills/feathers (craft stores carry feathers)

- sandpaper

- bottle of ink

- water

- scissors

- glue

- Optional to "quill" pen: calligraphy pen, fountain pen, or gel pen

PRACTICE MAKES PERFECT

Daily writing and penmanship were important in colonial schools. Pencils were expensive, so most students had to write using a quill pen. The pens were made from goose or turkey feathers. The quills were sharpened with a knife to make a point. Students dipped the quill pens in bottles of ink continually as they wrote. Students had to copy the alphabet and sentences over and over again until the teacher was happy with their penmanship. Young students were allowed to use lined paper to practice, but older students were expected to write neatly and straight on unlined paper. The ink was messy, so after the students finished writing, they had to use blotter paper to soak up the excess ink.

TYPICAL HANDWRITING STYLE OF THE 1600s

Calligraphy by Debra Ferreboeuf

EMC 3709 · Colonial America · ©2003 by Evan-Moor Corp.

THE FIRST SCHOOL BOOKS

Students make a hornbook, a paddle-shaped board to which a page of information is attached.

STEPS TO FOLLOW

1. Distribute page 62. Read the information about hornbooks with students.

2. Students cut out the hornbook pattern. They glue the hornbook to tagboard and cut around the shape.

3. On the blank side of the tagboard, instruct students to use black ballpoint pens or fine-tipped marking pens to write a sample lesson. You may wish to write this example on the chalkboard for students to copy:

> a e i o u ab eb ib ob ub
>
> eat ean eal eam eak
>
> I II III IV V VI VII VIII IX X
>
> Charity begins at home.

4. Have students trim a piece of transparency film to the size of the hornbook and use transparent tape to attach it over the sample lesson.

5. Have students punch a hole in the handle of the hornbook and attach a loop of string or yarn long enough to fit around their neck.

MATERIALS

- page 62, reproduced for each student
- 8½" x 11" (21.5 x 28 cm) tagboard
- scissors
- transparency film or scraps of laminate
- glue
- transparent tape
- black ballpoint pen or marking pen
- hole punch
- string or yarn

©2003 by Evan-Moor Corp. • EMC 3709 • Colonial America

HORNBOOK PATTERN

In colonial times, paper was scarce and expensive. Most students did not have textbooks. The main learning tool was the hornbook. The hornbook was invented to protect the paper on which children's lessons were printed.

The hornbook was a flat board with a handle. A piece of paper with information on it was pasted to the board. The lessons usually contained letter combinations, Roman numerals, and the Lord's Prayer. The board was covered with a piece of cattle horn cut so thin that the lessons could be read through it.

The handles of hornbooks had a hole drilled in them, through which a cord could be strung. Colonial students often wore the hornbook around their necks so it was handy for lessons.

EMC 3709 · Colonial America · ©2003 by Evan-Moor Corp.

Note: Reproduce this page for students to use with the "Daily Schedule" activity, as described on page 56.

DAILY SCHEDULE

Children in colonial America had a very demanding schedule. They were expected to do many chores to help the family. By the age of three or four, children were assigned "jobs" around the house and farm. By the age of five or six, children worked with their parents. Girls learned how to cook, sew, make candles, knit, and work in the garden. Boys learned how to plant crops, hunt, fish, and tan hides. If the father had a trade, such as being a blacksmith, the boys in the family worked in the family business by the time they were about seven. Children worked before and after school. There was little time left over for play.

Colonial Student's Daily Schedule

A.M.		P.M.	
4:00	do chores	12:00	lunch
5:00	eat breakfast	1:00	math
6:00	walk to school	2:00	learn manners
7:00	school begins	3:00	copy sentences
8:00	recite poems	4:00	walk home
9:00	read from the Bible	5:00	do chores
10:00	recess	6:00	supper
11:00	penmanship	7:00	homework
		8:00	bedtime

_____'s Daily Schedule

A.M.		P.M.	
4:00	_____	12:00	_____
5:00	_____	1:00	_____
6:00	_____	2:00	_____
7:00	_____	3:00	_____
8:00	_____	4:00	_____
9:00	_____	5:00	_____
10:00	_____	6:00	_____
11:00	_____	7:00	_____
_____	_____	8:00	_____

©2003 by Evan-Moor Corp. • EMC 3709 • Colonial America

Pocket 7

WORK

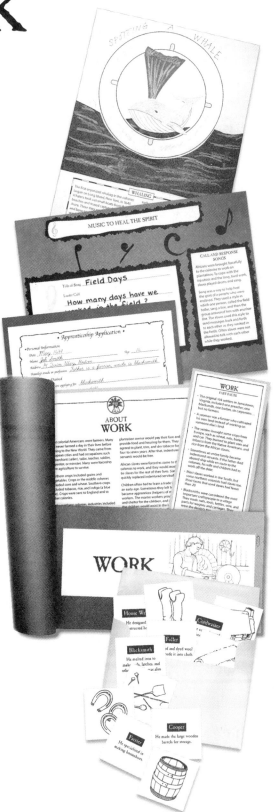

FAST FACTS

Make the bookmark about work in colonial America, following the directions on page 2. Students read and share interesting facts about work. Use the Fast Facts bookmark for a quick review during transition times throughout the day.

ABOUT

Reproduce this page for students. Read and discuss the important information to remember. Incorporate library and multimedia resources that are available.

ACTIVITIES

Students learn the unusual names for master craftspeople when they play a memory game using colonial trade cards.

Students pretend to be young colonial men and women who are applying for a job with a master. They review the trade cards to decide on a trade, and then they complete the application form.

Reproduce this page for students. Students read about how the slaves coped while they worked by making up songs in the call-and-response style. Students then follow directions to make up their own song. Provide 9" x 12" (23 x 30.5 cm) construction paper, scissors, and glue for each student to mount the information and the song they created. You may wish to create the call-and-response songs as a class before students attempt individual songs.

Whales have always been big, and whaling was big business in colonial New England. Students create a layered drawing of a whale viewed through a spyglass.

EMC 3709 · Colonial America · ©2003 by Evan-Moor Corp.

WORK

FAST FACTS

- The original 104 settlers in Jamestown, Virginia, included one preacher, one blacksmith, one barber, six carpenters… but no farmers.

- A yeoman was a farmer who cultivated his own land instead of working on someone else's land.

- The settlers brought some crops from Europe, such as wheat, oats, barley, and rye. They learned to plant corn and tobacco from the Native Americans, and rice from the African slaves.

- Sometimes an entire family became indentured servants. If the father died aboard ship while en route to the colonies, his wife and children had to work off the debt.

- Most slaves worked in the South, but some northern colonists had slaves too. Most farms that used slaves had fewer than 20.

- Blacksmiths were considered the most important craftspeople to a village. They made nails, tools, kettles, wire, and parts for wagons and carriages. They were the dentists too.

- Hunting whales meant big money. Their oil was needed for lamps.

- Other colonial jobs included brewer (beer maker), wig maker, papermaker, rope maker, glassmaker, and silversmith.

©2003 by Evan-Moor Corp. • EMC 3709

ABOUT
WORK

Most colonial Americans were farmers. Many had never farmed a day in their lives before coming to the New World. They came from European cities and had occupations such as merchant (seller), tailor, teacher, soldier, carpenter, or minister. Many were forced to learn agriculture to survive.

Northern crops included grains and vegetables. Crops in the middle colonies included corn and wheat. Southern crops included tobacco, rice, and indigo (a blue dye). Crops were sent to England and to other colonies.

In the northern colonies, industries included fishing, whaling, and shipbuilding. In the middle colonies, industries included dairy farming and raising animals for meat. Lumber production and mining became large industries in many colonies.

The wealthiest people were often public officials, farm or plantation owners, merchants, doctors, lawyers, or ministers. Middle-class men were often shoemakers or cabinetmakers. Middle-class women made candles, soap, and clothes for their families and also to sell to others. Men and some women ran shops. Poorer people had the hardest jobs. Many were laborers, sailors, or servants.

Indentured servants were people who wanted to come to the New World but could not afford the ocean voyage. A southern plantation owner would pay their fare and provide food and housing for them. They agreed to plant, trim, and dry tobacco for four to seven years. After that, indentured servants would be free.

African slaves were forced to come to the colonies to work, and they would most likely be slaves for the rest of their lives. Slavery quickly replaced indentured servitude.

Children often had to learn a trade (job) at an early age. Sometimes they left home to become apprentices (helpers) of master workers. The master workers provided food and shelter for the children, and in exchange, the children would assist in the labor. They learned skills that would allow them to work on their own one day.

EMC 3709 · Colonial America · ©2003 by Evan-Moor Corp.

COLONIAL TRADE CARDS

As the villages grew, so grew the need for more skilled workers. Every village had master craftspeople that set up shops to make and sell their products. The master craftspeople supervised the work and training of apprentices. Apprentices were young men who lived and worked alongside the masters to learn the trades.

By playing a memory game, students will learn about 12 different names of craftspeople that were once commonplace in colonial America.

STEPS TO FOLLOW

1. Have students study pages 68 and 69, which list the craftspeople and the products they made in colonial America.

2. Instruct students to glue construction paper to the back of pages 68 and 69 to make them sturdier.

3. When dry, have students cut the pages apart to make 24 cards. There will be 12 craftspeople cards and 12 product cards.

4. Students mix up the cards and then put them facedown on a table.

5. They try to match up the craftspeople with the products that they made. You may want them to play this memory game with a partner.

6. Have students store their colonial trade cards in an envelope.

MATERIALS

- pages 68 and 69, reproduced for each student
- two 9" x 12" (23 x 30.5 cm) sheets of construction paper
- scissors
- glue
- envelope

©2003 by Evan-Moor Corp. • EMC 3709 • Colonial America

COLONIAL TRADE CARDS

Blacksmith

He melted iron to make nails, latches, and other tools. He was also the dentist.

Cooper

He made the large wooden barrels for storage.

Cordwainer

He cut and sewed shoes by hand.

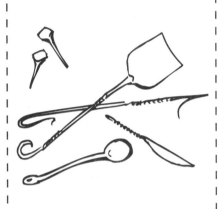

Farrier

He specialized in making horseshoes.

Fuller

He cleaned and dyed wool and then made it into cloth.

House Wright

He designed and constructed houses.

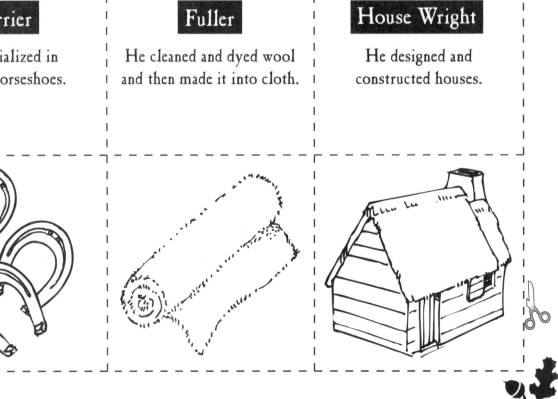

EMC 3709 · Colonial America · ©2003 by Evan-Moor Corp.

COLONIAL TRADE CARDS

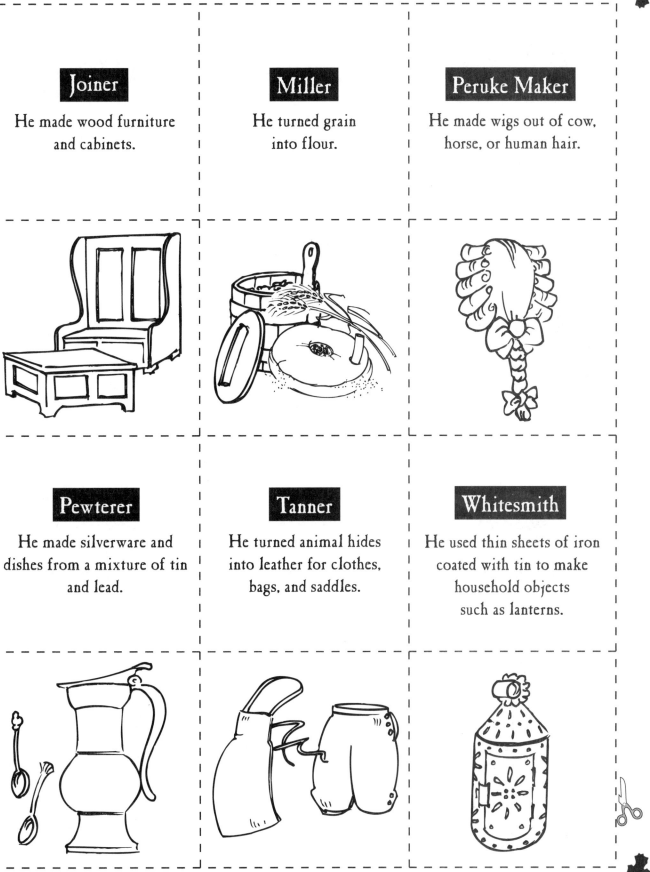

Joiner

He made wood furniture
and cabinets.

Miller

He turned grain
into flour.

Peruke Maker

He made wigs out of cow,
horse, or human hair.

Pewterer

He made silverware and
dishes from a mixture of tin
and lead.

Tanner

He turned animal hides
into leather for clothes,
bags, and saddles.

Whitesmith

He used thin sheets of iron
coated with tin to make
household objects
such as lanterns.

©2003 by Evan-Moor Corp. • EMC 3709 • Colonial America

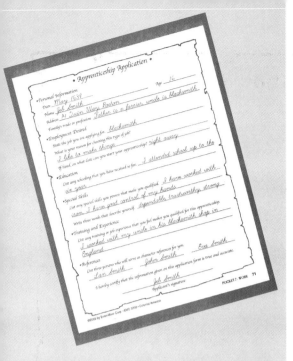

MATERIALS

- page 71, reproduced for each student
- 9" x 12" (23 x 30.5 cm) construction paper
- writing paper
- pencil or pen
- scissors
- glue

AN APPRENTICESHIP

Students learned about the different trades in colonial America when they played the "Colonial Trade Cards" memory game. Now it is time for the students to decide which occupation interests them the most. They fill out a job application form to become an apprentice with a master craftsperson.

STEPS TO FOLLOW

1. Have students review the "Colonial Trade Cards" from the last activity. Instruct them each to choose a job they would like to have had in colonial America.

2. Hand out the job application form from page 71. Students are to pretend they are young colonial men and women who are applying for a job with a master.

   Discuss skills and personal qualities that master craftspeople would be looking for in their apprentices. You may want the students to incorporate some factual information about themselves on the application form.

3. The students fill out the application form. Remind them to write neatly and to write confidently about their skills so they are the ones chosen to be apprentices.

4. Instruct students to cut out the application form and glue it to construction paper to make it sturdier.

5. Share the job applications as a class. You may want to have students "interview" with "master craftspeople" in your class.

EMC 3709 · Colonial America · ©2003 by Evan-Moor Corp.

◆ Apprenticeship Application ◆

◆ Personal Information

Date _____

Name _____ Age _____

Address_____

Family's trade or profession _____

◆ Employment Desired

State the job you are applying for. _____

What is your reason for choosing this type of job?

_____

If hired, on what date can you start your apprenticeship? _____

◆ Education

List any schooling that you have received so far. _____

_____

◆ Special Skills

List any special skills you possess that make you qualified. _____

_____

Write three words that describe yourself. _____

◆ Training and Experience

List any training or job experience that you feel makes you qualified for this apprenticeship.

_____

_____

◆ References

List three persons who will serve as character references for you.

_____   _____   _____

I hereby certify that the information given on this application form is true and accurate.

_____

Applicant's signature

©2003 by Evan-Moor Corp. · EMC 3709 · Colonial America

MUSIC TO HEAL THE SPIRIT

1. Read the information about call-and-response songs.

2. Pretend you are a field holler and write a two-line verse of a song of hope to your friends and family working beside you out in the fields.

> Here is an example of a call-and-response song:
>
> **Leader:** Children, are you ready and willing to roam?
>
> **Group:** We're ready and willing to journey back home.
>
> Notice there is a hidden message in this song. Maybe the slaves are getting ready to run away from the plantation.

3. Write the first line of the song below. You may write the message in the form of a question.

4. Write another line to answer the first one. You may find this easier if you have the two lines rhyme. The second line is what the group sings back to the leader. You may want to set the verses to music.

5. Cut out the song and information box. Glue them to construction paper.

CALL-AND-RESPONSE SONGS

Africans were brought forcefully to the colonies to work on plantations. To cope with the injustices and the long, hard work, slaves played drums and sang.

Song was a way to help heal the spirit of a people who were enslaved. They used a style in which one person, called the field holler, sang a line, and then the group answered him with another line. The slaves used this style to send messages back and forth to each other as they worked in the fields. Often slaves were not allowed to talk with each other while they worked.

Title of Song _____

Leader Call

_____

_____

_____

Group Response

_____

_____

_____

 EMC 3709 · Colonial America · ©2003 by Evan-Moor Corp.

SPOTTING A WHALE

Whaling was a major industry in colonial America, particularly in Massachusetts. Students make a colorful picture of a whale viewed through a spyglass.

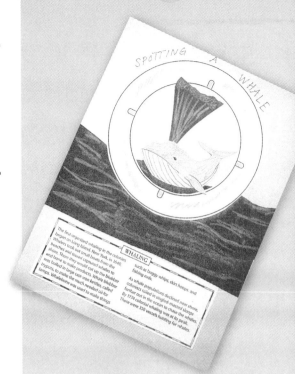

STEPS TO FOLLOW

1. Have students cut out the circular ring and information from page 74. Direct students to discard the interior circle and set the ring aside. The circular ring is the field of view of their colonial spyglass.

2. Direct students to glue the whaling information onto the bottom of the light-colored sheet of construction paper.

3. Have students cut "waves" made from blue construction paper and then glue them above the boxed information, to represent the ocean.

4. Direct students to draw a whale on the gray construction paper and cut it out.

5. Then have students cut out a waterspout for the whale, using blue construction paper.

6. Instruct students to glue the circular ring on top of the waves and then glue the whale and waterspout inside the ring. Then have students write the title "Spotting a Whale" at the top of the sheet.

MATERIALS

- page 74, reproduced for each student
- 9" x 12" (23 x 30.5 cm) light-colored construction paper
- blue construction paper scraps
- 4" x 4" (10 x 10 cm) gray construction paper
- pencil
- crayons or marking pens
- scissors
- glue

©2003 by Evan-Moor Corp. • EMC 3709 • Colonial America

SPOTTING A WHALE

WHALING

The first organized whaling in the colonies began on Long Island, New York, in 1640. Whalers took out small boats from the beaches and towed captured whales to shore. There they would cut up the blubber and bone to make products. Whale blubber was boiled in large cast-iron kettles, called trypots, to make the much needed oil for lamps. Whalebone was used to make things such as buggy whips, skirt hoops, and fishing rods.

As whale populations declined near shore, colonists sailed in singled-masted sloops farther out in the ocean to chase the whales. By 1774 colonial whaling was at its peak. There were 350 vessels hunting for whales.

EMC 3709 · Colonial America · ©2003 by Evan-Moor Corp.

Pocket 8

MEMORABLE PEOPLE

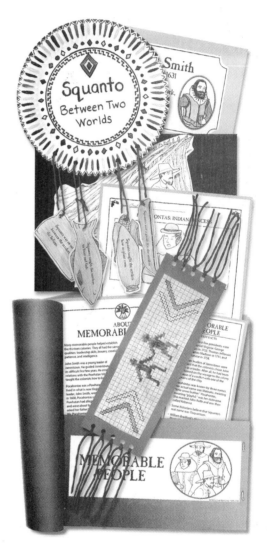

FAST FACTS

Memorable People . . . . **page 76**
Make the bookmark about memorable people in
colonial America, following the directions on
page 2. Students read and share interesting facts
about memorable people. Use the Fast Facts
bookmark for a quick review during transition times
throughout the day.

ABOUT

Memorable People . . . . **page 77**
Reproduce this page for students. Read and discuss
the important information to remember. Incorporate
library and multimedia resources that are available.

ACTIVITIES

John Smith: Hero of Jamestown . . . . . **pages 78 & 79**
Students read about how John Smith helped the
colonists survive the first year in a new colony. They
make a plaque in his honor.

Pocahontas: Indian Princess . . . . **pages 80 & 81**
Reproduce these pages for students. Have students
read the story of Pocahontas. Students then draw a
portrait of this legendary Indian princess and write
an acrostic poem using the letters of her name.

Squanto: Between Two Worlds . . . . . . **pages 82 & 83**
Students make a peacemaker's shield showing the
many ways in which Squanto was a lifeline for the
young Plymouth Colony.

William Bradford: "Let the Light Shine" . . . . **pages 84–86**
Plymouth's governor, William Bradford, believed his determined colony could be an inspiration to
other settlements. Students create a pop-up book dedicated to Bradford.

Roger Williams: Into the Woods . . . . **pages 87–89**
To ensure that Roger Williams survives the winter so he can found Providence, students create
a pull-tab shelter for him in the forest.

William Penn: Peacemaker . . . . **pages 90 & 91**
Students make a friendship belt similar to the one Chief Tamanend gave William Penn.

MEMORABLE
PEOPLE

©2003 by Evan-Moor Corp. • EMC 3709

MEMORABLE PEOPLE

FAST FACTS

- Four of the first five presidents were born in colonial Virginia: George Washington in 1732, Thomas Jefferson in 1743, James Madison in 1751, and James Monroe in 1758.

- The other leaders of Jamestown were surprised that the colonists chose John Smith as a leader. After all, he had been imprisoned on the voyage to the colony because of a conflict with one of the captains of the ship.

- Pocahontas was known by three names. Her actual name was Matoaka, meaning "little snow feather." Pocahontas, meaning "playful," was her nickname. She married John Rolfe and was then called Rebecca.

- Some historians believe that Squanto's real name was Tisquantum.

- William Bradford's *History of Plimoth Plantation, 1620-1647* was first published in 1856, almost 200 years after Bradford died in 1657.

- In 1636 Roger Williams, founder of Rhode Island, wrote a book called *A Key into the Language of America,* in which he attempted to translate Indian languages into English.

- William Penn was asked to leave Oxford University, in England, because he refused to go to the Church of England. He left his rich life behind to become a Quaker in his new colony in what is now called Pennsylvania.

©2003 by Evan-Moor Corp. • EMC 3709

ABOUT
MEMORABLE PEOPLE

Many memorable people helped establish the thirteen colonies. They all had the same qualities: leadership skills, bravery, creativity, patience, and intelligence.

John Smith was a young leader of Jamestown. He guided Jamestown through its difficult first few years. He established relations with the Powhatan tribe, who taught the colonists how to live off the land.

Pocahontas was a Powhatan Indian who lived in what is now Virginia. Jamestown's leader, John Smith, wrote in his journal that in 1608, Pocahontas saved his life. A group of Powhatan had allegedly captured John Smith and were about to kill him when Pocahontas asked her father to spare the white settler's life. Pocahontas helped the colonists and Native Americans cooperate.

Squanto was a Patuxet Indian who lived in the area that is now Massachusetts and Rhode Island. He spoke English well. Squanto joined the Wampanoag tribe and helped the Pilgrims to survive by teaching them how to plant corn and fish. Squanto was an interpreter for Governor William Bradford and Wampanoag Chief Massasoit when they agreed to a peace treaty in 1621.

William Bradford was a Pilgrim who came over on the *Mayflower* and helped found Plymouth. He was governor for 30 years and helped build up the colony. He wrote *History of Plimoth Plantation, 1620–1647*, the Pilgrims' story. Bradford was also one of the signers of the Mayflower Compact in 1620, and an organizer of the first harvest feast in 1621.

Roger Williams was a Massachusetts Puritan minister who had ideas that other Puritans disliked. He said the Indians should be paid for their land and that no one should be forced to believe in a certain religion. In 1636 Williams founded Providence, Rhode Island, as a haven for religious freedom and tolerance.

William Penn was a Quaker who founded Pennsylvania. The Quakers disagreed with the Church of England. Penn, like Roger Williams, said his colony was open to people of any faith. Quakers believed all people were equal—including women, blacks, and Native Americans. That was a very controversial idea at the time.

All these leaders of the colonies will be remembered for their achievements.

©2003 by Evan-Moor Corp. • EMC 3709 • Colonial America

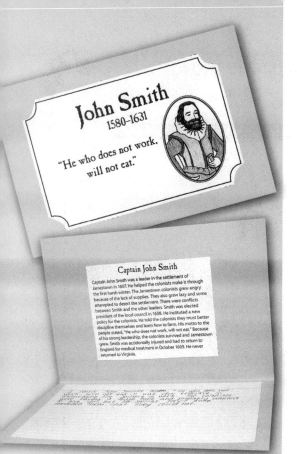

JOHN SMITH: HERO OF JAMESTOWN

Students make a plaque about John Smith and write a short paragraph explaining whether they think his motto for the settlement was a good one.

STEPS TO FOLLOW

1. Have students read the information about John Smith on page 79.

2. Direct students to fold the construction paper in half, cut out the plaque, and glue it to the front of the paper folder.

3. Students cut out the information about John Smith and glue it on the top inside section of the construction paper folder.

4. Students write a short paragraph on the index card about whether Smith's motto was effective. Do students think the motto would have motivated the colonists to stay in Jamestown?

5. Have students glue the index card to the bottom inside section of the construction paper folder.

MATERIALS

- page 79, reproduced for each student
- 9" x 12" (23 x 30.5 cm) construction paper
- 4" x 6" (10 x 15 cm) index card or writing paper
- pencil
- scissors
- glue

EMC 3709 · Colonial America · ©2003 by Evan-Moor Corp.

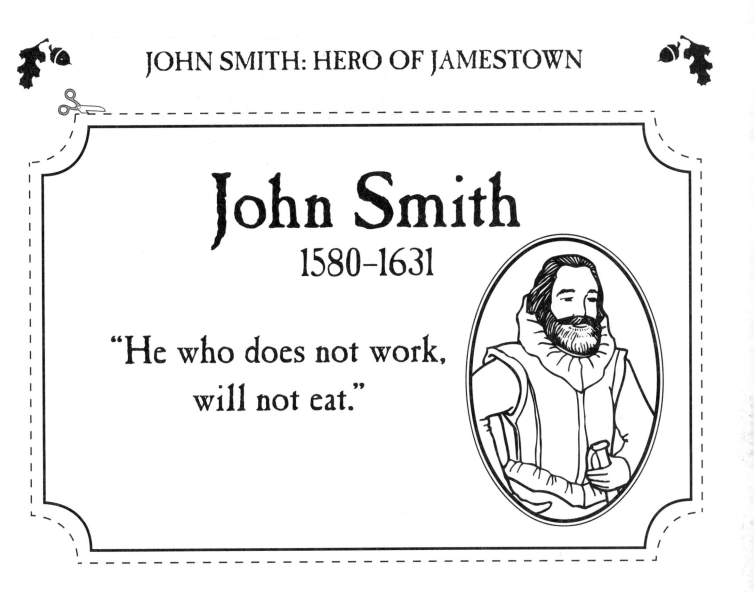

John Smith
1580–1631

"He who does not work,
will not eat."

Captain John Smith

Captain John Smith was a leader in the settlement of Jamestown in 1607. He helped the colonists make it through the first harsh winter. The Jamestown colonists grew angry because of the lack of supplies. They also grew lazy, and some attempted to desert the settlement. There were conflicts between Smith and the other leaders. Smith was elected president of the local council in 1608. He instituted a new policy for the colonists. He told the colonists they must better discipline themselves and learn how to farm. His motto to the people stated, "He who does not work, will not eat." Because of his strong leadership, the colonists survived and Jamestown grew. Smith was accidentally injured and had to return to England for medical treatment in October 1609. He never returned to Virginia.

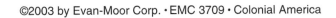

Name: _____

POCAHONTAS: INDIAN PRINCESS

Pocahontas is one of those legendary figures of colonial America. Her story has been portrayed in books and movies.

The famous Indian princess was born in 1595 with the name Matoaka. She was the daughter of Powhatan, chief of the entire Algonquin nation in the region of present-day Virginia. She met the English when the Native Americans took their captain, John Smith, captive. Captain John Smith reported to others later that, just when he was about to be killed, a young Indian girl saved his life. She supposedly threw herself across Smith to stop her father's warriors from beating him to death. Some say she was then appointed his "protector" so that Powhatan could stay informed about the English.

For several years she visited the English settlement of Jamestown, bringing them food and news from her tribe. The English nicknamed her Pocahontas. After John Smith left the colony, another captain, Samuel Argall, kidnapped her and took her to Jamestown to live. He planned to exchange the chief's daughter for some English prisoners. During the several months Pocahontas was held hostage, she learned English and became a Christian. She was made to live with Reverend Alexander Whitaker and learn the manners of an English lady. She met an Englishman, John Rolfe, at this time. They fell in love and were married. She was given the English name Rebecca. They had a son, Thomas, and left for England the next year.

John Rolfe and Rebecca went to England to encourage the English to invest in Virginia. She was hailed as an Indian princess and was presented to the king and queen in 1617. Pocahontas got very sick in England. They say she had pneumonia or tuberculosis. She died in March of 1617.

Whether she was called Matoaka, Pocahontas, or Rebecca, she will always be remembered as a courageous young woman. She was a vital link between the Native Americans and the English settlers.

EMC 3709 · Colonial America · ©2003 by Evan-Moor Corp.

POCAHONTAS: INDIAN PRINCESS

_____
title

P
O
C
A
H
O
N
T
A
S

SQUANTO: BETWEEN TWO WORLDS

Students make a peacemaker's shield showing the many things that Squanto did for the settlers: teaching them how to plant corn, teaching them how to hunt and fish, acting as a guide in the wilderness, and acting as a translator and interpreter when William Bradford and Chief Massasoit brokered a Pilgrim/Indian peace treaty.

STEPS TO FOLLOW

1. Review the information on Squanto on the "About Memorable People" page.

2. Have students lightly color and cut out the patterns on page 83. They punch holes as shown on the patterns.

3. Direct students to write the title "Squanto: Between Two Worlds" on a paper plate. Have them decorate the plate and then punch four holes near the bottom.

4. Instruct students to use raffia to tie the corn, fish, canoe, and peace treaty to the paper plate.

MATERIALS

- page 83, reproduced for each student
- small white paper plate
- pencil
- crayons or marking pens
- scissors
- hole punch
- raffia

EMC 3709 · Colonial America · ©2003 by Evan-Moor Corp.

SQUANTO: BETWEEN TWO WORLDS

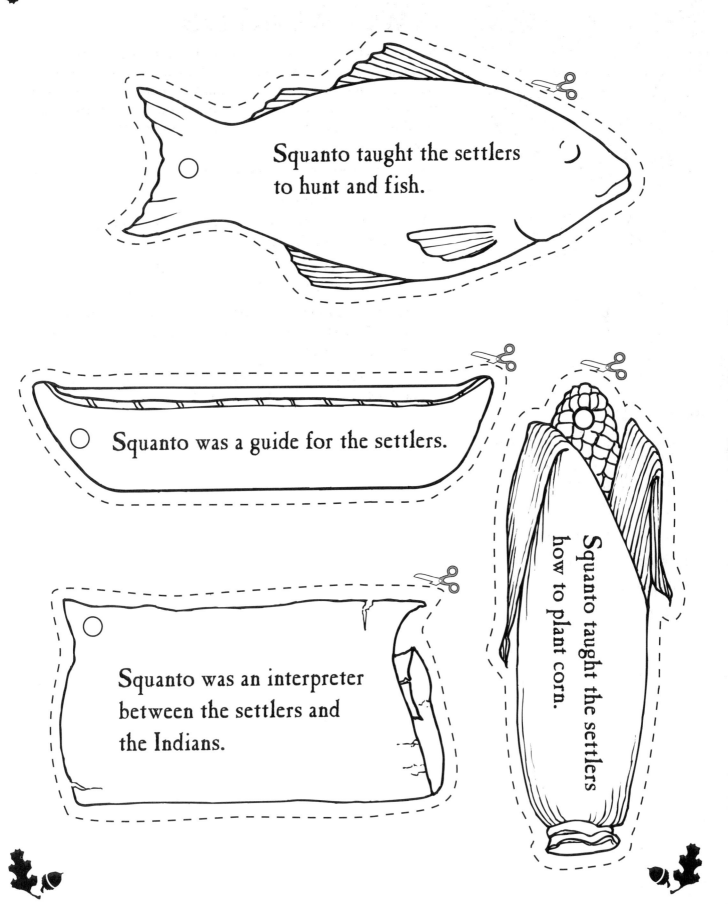

Squanto taught the settlers to hunt and fish.

Squanto was a guide for the settlers.

Squanto was an interpreter between the settlers and the Indians.

Squanto taught the settlers how to plant corn.

WILLIAM BRADFORD: "LET THE LIGHT SHINE"

As we all know, the Pilgrims settled in Massachusetts. William Bradford became governor of the new colony. Governor William Bradford wrote of his colony: "as one small candle may light a thousand, so the light here kindled hath shone unto many, yea, in some sort, to our whole nation."

Students make a pop-up book about William Bradford and his famous quote.

STEPS TO FOLLOW

1. Review the information about William Bradford presented on the "About Memorable People" page.

2. Direct students to read Bradford's quote on the pop-up book on page 85. On the writing lines provided, have students write about what they think the quote means.

3. Have students make the pop-up book.

   a. Cut and fold the pop-up pattern. Pull tabs to the inside, reversing the fold.

   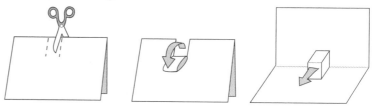

   b. Cut out the candle from page 86. Glue it to a scrap of yellow construction paper and cut around the edges. Add yellow tissue paper to the flame.

   c. Put glue on the tab and press the candle pattern on.

   d. Cut out the picture of Bradford from page 86 and glue it to the pop-up pattern.

   e. Fold the large piece of construction paper. Place the pop-up pattern in the folded paper. Place glue on the pop-up pattern, close the construction paper, and press firmly.

   f. Flip the book over and follow the same steps in gluing the other side. Allow it to dry.

4. Share the meanings of the quote as a class.

MATERIALS

- page 85 reproduced for each student, and page 86 reproduced for each pair of students
- 9" x 12" (23 x 30.5 cm) yellow construction paper
- yellow construction paper scraps
- yellow tissue paper scraps
- pencil
- crayons or marking pens
- scissors
- glue

EMC 3709 · Colonial America · ©2003 by Evan-Moor Corp.

WILLIAM BRADFORD: "LET THE LIGHT SHINE" POP-UP PATTERN

"as one small candle
may light a thousand, so the
light here kindled hath shone
unto many, yea, in some sort,
to our whole nation."

glue portrait here

fold

fold

fold

glue candle here

fold

William Bradford's quote meant...

____

____

____

____

____

"LET THE LIGHT SHINE" PATTERNS

William Bradford
1590–1657

"LET THE LIGHT SHINE" PATTERNS

William Bradford
1590–1657

EMC 3709 · Colonial America · ©2003 by Evan-Moor Corp.

ROGER WILLIAMS: INTO THE WOODS

It was January 1636 and bitingly cold when Roger Williams fled Boston, Massachusetts. But before he could found Providence, he had to endure the winter.

Students build a pull-tab shelter to protect Roger Williams from the harsh New England elements.

Roger Williams

Roger Williams, a Puritan minister, believed that all people should worship freely. He also believed that Puritan leaders should be respectful to the Algonquin Indians. His views went against those of the local leaders. They wanted Williams to change his views, but he refused. They were going to send him back to England, so Roger Williams fled into the wilderness with the help of the Algonquin. A year later, Williams established a new colony in Providence, Rhode Island, where government and religion were separate and all people could worship freely.

STEPS TO FOLLOW

1. Review the life of Roger Williams on the "About Memorable People" page.

2. Have students color and cut out the shelter on page 88. They glue the shelter to construction paper and cut around the edges.

3. Direct students to cut the slit through the shelter and construction paper.

4. Have students color and cut out the the pull-tab figure of Williams on page 89. Glue it to the small piece of construction paper and cut around the edges.

5. Direct them to insert the pull-tab of Williams into the slit in the shelter.

6. Have students cut out and glue the information about Roger Williams to the bottom of the construction paper.

7. Read the information on Roger Williams. Discuss what it would be like to endure a whole winter alone with only a temporary shelter to protect you from the elements.

MATERIALS

- pages 88 and 89, reproduced for each student
- 9" x 12" (23 x 30.5 cm) construction paper
- 6" x 9" (15 x 23 cm) construction paper
- pencil
- crayons or marking pens
- scissors
- glue

ROGER WILLIAMS: INTO THE WOODS

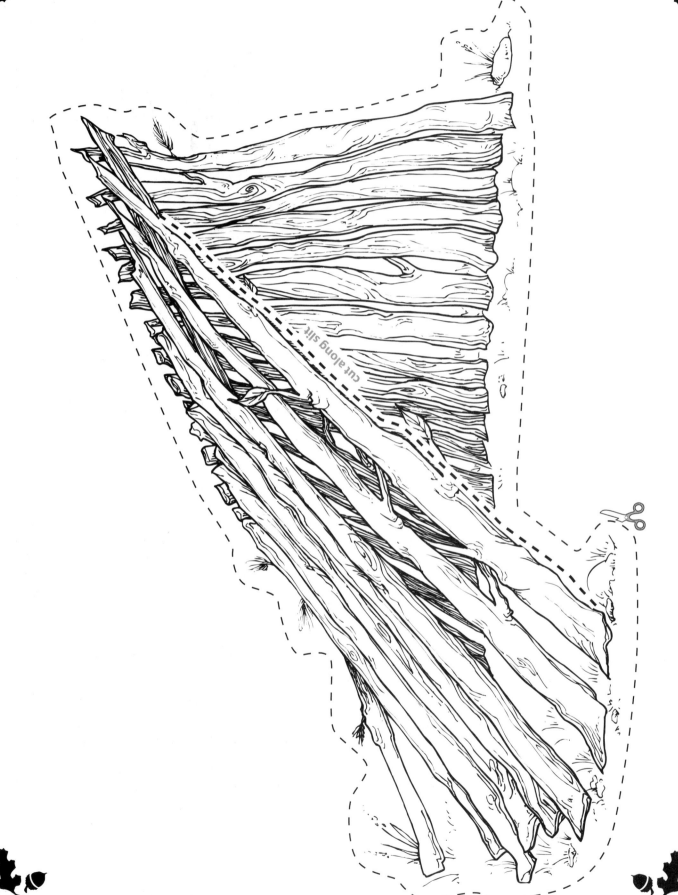

cut along slit

 EMC 3709 · Colonial America · ©2003 by Evan-Moor Corp.

Roger Williams

Roger Williams, a Puritan minister, believed that all people should worship freely. He also believed that Puritan leaders should be respectful to the Algonquin Indians. His views went against those of the local leaders. They wanted Williams to change his views, but he refused. They were going to send him back to England, so Roger Williams fled into the wilderness with the help of the Algonquin. A year later, Williams established a new colony in Providence, Rhode Island, where government and religion were separate and all people could worship freely.

©2003 by Evan-Moor Corp. • EMC 3709 • Colonial America

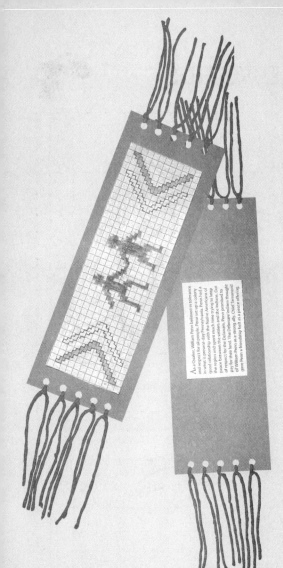

WILLIAM PENN: PEACEMAKER

Students make a friendship belt similar to the one Chief Tamanend gave William Penn as a peace offering.

STEPS TO FOLLOW

1. Share with students the information about William Penn and his relationship with the Delaware Indians.

2. Have students read the information and study the example of the friendship belt on page 91.

3. Direct students to re-create the friendship belt on the graph paper strip provided. They are to include two stick figures shaking hands in the center of the belt. Students then color in the squares to make the belt look beaded.

4. Instruct students to cut out the belt and glue it to the construction paper strip.

5. Then students add fringe to the ends of the belt by using a hole punch and yarn.

6. Have students cut out and glue the information box to the back of the belt.

MATERIALS

- page 91, reproduced for each student
- 4" x 12" (10 x 30.5 cm) construction paper
- pencil
- crayons or marking pens
- scissors
- yarn or raffia
- glue
- hole punch

EMC 3709 · Colonial America · ©2003 by Evan-Moor Corp.

WILLIAM PENN: PEACEMAKER

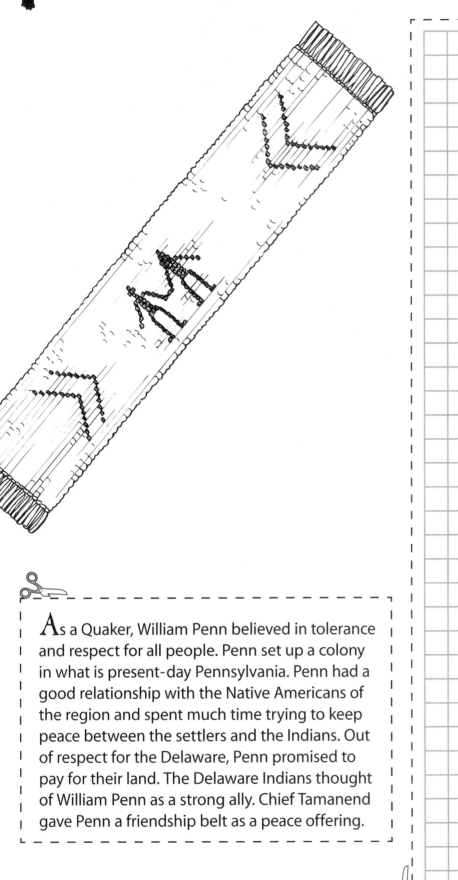

As a Quaker, William Penn believed in tolerance and respect for all people. Penn set up a colony in what is present-day Pennsylvania. Penn had a good relationship with the Native Americans of the region and spent much time trying to keep peace between the settlers and the Indians. Out of respect for the Delaware, Penn promised to pay for their land. The Delaware Indians thought of William Penn as a strong ally. Chief Tamanend gave Penn a friendship belt as a peace offering.

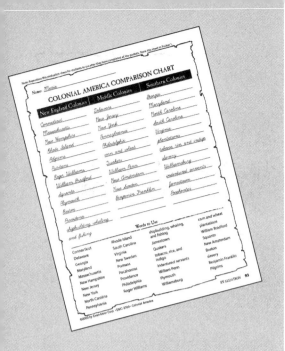

COLONIAL AMERICA COMPARISON CHART

Now that students have completed all the pockets, you may test their knowledge of the thirteen colonies by having them fill out this Colonial America Comparison Chart.

STEPS TO FOLLOW

1. Give students the list of colonial American words. Direct them to look throughout the pockets for the words given. You may want to have the students highlight the words as they find them.

2. Instruct students to fill in the words on the Colonial America Comparison Chart. You may wish to have students do this individually or in small groups.

3. Give the students the correct answers. You may choose to have students do a self-correction. An answer key has been provided for you on page 96.

4. Have students store the comparison chart in Pocket 1.

MATERIALS

- page 93, reproduced for each student
- pencil
- highlighter pen

EMC 3709 • Colonial America • ©2003 by Evan-Moor Corp.

Name: _____

COLONIAL AMERICA COMPARISON CHART

New England Colonies	Middle Colonies	Southern Colonies

Words to Use

Connecticut	Rhode Island	shipbuilding, whaling, and fishing	corn and wheat
Delaware	South Carolina	Jamestown	plantations
Georgia	Virginia	Quakers	William Bradford
Maryland	New Sweden	tobacco, rice, and indigo	Squanto
Massachusetts	Puritans	indentured servants	New Amsterdam
New Hampshire	Pocahontas	William Penn	Boston
New Jersey	Providence	Plymouth	slavery
New York	Philadelphia	Williamsburg	Benjamin Franklin
North Carolina	Roger Williams		Pilgrims
Pennsylvania			

EVALUATION **93**

COLONIAL AMERICA REFLECTION SHEET

Name: _____ Date: _____

Directions: Please fill out this sheet after you have completed your book.

1. When I look through my colonial America book, I feel _____

   because _____

2. The project I liked doing the most was the _____

   because _____

3. The project I liked doing the least was the _____

   because _____

4. Three things I am most proud of in my colonial America book are _____

   _____

   _____

   _____

5. Three things I would do differently to improve my colonial America book are _____

   _____

   _____

   _____

6. Three facts that I learned about colonial America that I did not know before doing this project are

   _____

   _____

   _____

7. Name three achievements of colonial America. How has each of these achievements affected our lives today?

   Achievement 1: _____

   _____

   Achievement 2: _____

   _____

   Achievement 3: _____

   _____

 EMC 3709 • Colonial America • ©2003 by Evan-Moor Corp.

COLONIAL AMERICA EVALUATION SHEET

Directions: Look through all the pockets and evaluate how well the activities were completed. Use the following point system:

6 outstanding	5 excellent	4 very good	3 satisfactory	2 some effort	1 little effort	0 no effort

Self-Evaluation	Peer Evaluation	Teacher Evaluation

Self-Evaluation

Name: _____

____ completed assignments

____ followed directions

____ had correct information

____ edited writing

____ showed creativity

____ displayed neatness

____ added color

____ **total points**

Comments: _____

_____

Peer Evaluation

Name: _____

____ completed assignments

____ followed directions

____ had correct information

____ edited writing

____ showed creativity

____ displayed neatness

____ added color

____ **total points**

Comments: _____

_____

Teacher Evaluation

____ completed assignments

____ followed directions

____ had correct information

____ edited writing

____ showed creativity

____ displayed neatness

____ added color

____ **total points**

____ **grade**

Comments: _____

_____

Page 14

Note: Reproduce this page for students to use with "The Thirteen Colonies Word Search" activity, as described on page 4.

Name: _____

THE THIRTEEN COLONIES WORD SEARCH

```
P O N M A S S A C H U S E T T S
E K E C H T H S O U N N G E O R
N R W D E L A W A R E E P U M T
N D W B C Q C U B V W W T V A U
S Y A B Z E D G H K Z C A W R S
Y L A F I V L R C A I M U G P I
V A S D E D Y O L R K J J P Y I
A I N E W Y B O R Z U S L N Q E
N E T R W A L O N E G H I K I N
I D C E Y I A H E R G I Z A R N
A O N D N M N P A W O R N A T O
N H M A R Y L A N D N E W R U C
Y R A A N I L O R A C H T R O N
  G E O R G I A T N E W N O R T H
  G Y N E W M A S S V A N U C X J
```

Words to Find

Connecticut	New Hampshire	Rhode Island
Delaware	New Jersey	South Carolina
Georgia	New York	Virginia
Maryland	North Carolina	
Massachusetts	Pennsylvania	

Page 42

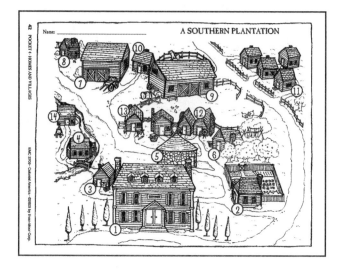

42 POCKET 4 · HOMES AND VILLAGES

Name: _____

A SOUTHERN PLANTATION

EMC 3709 · Colonial America · ©2003 by Evan-Moor Corp.

Page 93

Note: Reproduce this evaluation sheet for students to use after they have completed all the pockets. Store this sheet in Pocket 1.

Name: _____

COLONIAL AMERICA COMPARISON CHART

New England Colonies	Middle Colonies	Southern Colonies
Connecticut	Delaware	Georgia
Massachusetts	New Jersey	Maryland
New Hampshire	New York	North Carolina
Rhode Island	Pennsylvania	South Carolina
Pilgrims	Philadelphia	Virginia
Puritans	corn and wheat	plantations
Roger Williams	Quakers	tobacco, rice, and indigo
William Bradford	William Penn	slavery
Squanto	New Amsterdam	Williamsburg
Plymouth	New Sweden	indentured servants
Boston	Benjamin Franklin	Jamestown
Providence		Pocahontas
shipbuilding, whaling, and fishing		

Words to Use

Connecticut	Rhode Island	shipbuilding, whaling, and fishing	corn and wheat
Delaware	South Carolina	Jamestown	plantations
Georgia	Virginia	Quakers	William Bradford
Maryland	New Sweden	tobacco, rice, and indigo	Squanto
Massachusetts	Puritans	indentured servants	New Amsterdam
New Hampshire	Pocahontas	William Penn	Boston
New Jersey	Providence	Plymouth	slavery
New York	Philadelphia	Williamsburg	Benjamin Franklin
North Carolina	Roger Williams		Pilgrims
Pennsylvania			

©2003 by Evan-Moor Corp. · EMC 3709 · Colonial America   EVALUATION 93